Carrie Bloomston

THE LITTLE SPARK

30 Ways to Ignite Your Creativity

stashBOOKS®
an imprint of C&T Publishing

Publisher:
Amy Marson

Creative Director:
Gailen Runge

Art Director/
Book Designer:
Kristy Zacharias

Editor:
Lynn Koolish

Technical Editor:
Teresa Stroin

Production
Coordinators:
Jenny Davis and
Freesia Pearson
Blizard

Production Editor:
Katie Van Amburg

Cover Illustrator:
Zinnia Heinzmann

Photo Assistant:
Mary Peyton Peppo

Photography by
Jill McNamara,
unless otherwise
noted

Published by Stash Books, an imprint of C&T Publishing, Inc.,
P.O. Box 1456, Lafayette, CA 94549

Attention Teachers: C&T Publishing, Inc., encourages you to use this book as a text for teaching. Contact us at 800-284-1114 or www.ctpub.com for lesson plans and information about the C&T Creative Troupe.

Library of Congress Cataloging-in-Publication Data

Bloomston, Carrie, 1972-

The little spark : 30 ways to ignite your creativity / Carrie Bloomston.

pages cm

ISBN 978-1-60705-960-8 (soft cover)

1. Creation (Literary, artistic, etc.) 2. Inspiration. 3. Creative ability. I. Title.

BF408.B544 2014

153.3'5--dc23

2014009342

Printed in China

10 9 8 7 6 5 4 3 2 1

For Lucie, Ronan, and Kris—you are my everything. I endeavor to make you proud.

For Mom and Dad—thank you for loving me so well.

For Dicki Arn—thank you for holding my tiny Spark in your gentle hands for those early and important seven years.

Many of the photos were taken by my stellar photographer, Jill McNamara. She has magic in her camera, and you can feel the craft in her images. She is a delight to work with. With Jill it doesn't feel like work—it's just easy. Check out her website, jillmcnamara.com.

This book is filled with inspiring images because my beautiful, talented, and willing friends showed up for me when I asked. As my favorite fortune cookie says, "He climbs highest who helps another up." Thank you, my friends, for helping me.

I'd also like to thank my friend Elaina Verhoff for editing the whole book and helping make it better.

Finally, thank you to everyone at Stash Books—for believing in me and for making such a beautiful book.

ADDITIONAL PHOTOGRAPHY BY:

Jenny Dawson blue batik fabric, Singer sewing machine (pages 4 and 5)
Amber Corcoran Janome sewing machine (page 5)
Logan Milliken metalwork (page 5)
Asya Palatova pastels (page 5)
Photospin stairway (page 24), traffic light (page 25), splatter (page 28), Indian market (page 52), teas (page 55), fire (page 88)
Diane Pedersen, C&T Publishing quilt (page 103), miscellaneous fabrics
Nissa Brehmer, C&T Publishing woman (page 58), lemon (page 114)

CONTENTS

HOW TO USE THIS BOOK

This book is an interactive workbook designed to help you step into a creative life through engaging exercises, fun activities, inspirational images, and motivating ideas. It will help you get

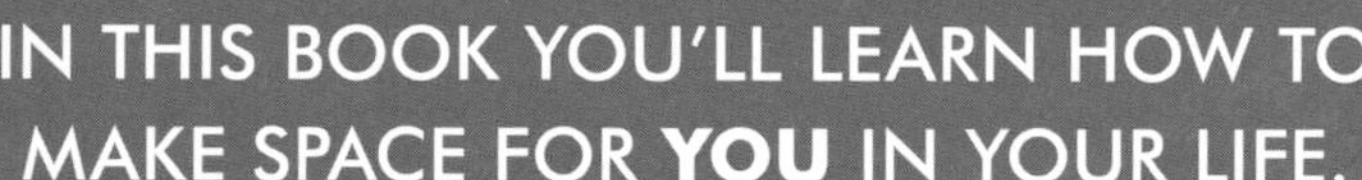
IN THIS BOOK YOU'LL LEARN HOW TO
MAKE SPACE FOR **YOU** IN YOUR LIFE.

to know yourself and your desires. You will learn what your little Spark of passion, of creativity, looks like, how to capture it, and how to make space for it in your life.

Living a creative life means more than being an artist, writer, quilter, crafter, or chef. It is a way of living life with curiosity and openness. It means thinking from your heart, thinking for yourself, and thinking outside the box. In this book you'll learn how to make space for *you* in your life. You'll step into who you want to become and remember who you already are.

This is a journey into wonder and yourself. There are 30 Sparks, or chapters, in this book. You can do one a day for a month. You can do them one a week for 30 weeks. You can do them at any time and in any order. Do what works for you. As you explore each Spark, you'll be motivated, exhilarated, and brought in touch with yourself. You'll grow more confident about your ability and be ready to receive the gifts of a creative life—joy, connection, meaning, and contentment—gifts that come from doing something with passion. Your little Spark will be a happy bonfire, burning brightly in you. It will change your life.

CREATE

INTRODUCTION

THE LITTLE SPARK is a beginning, a seed, a whisper. It is an unanswered question—a nudge from your unconscious. It's a bit magical. It has a strange hold over you. It calls you with its siren song—yet you find a million ways to ignore it. You watch cooking shows on late-night television. You shop. You work. You nap. That is, until now.

Your creativity is like a pilot light—it's always on, even if you aren't using the stove. And like the pilot light, it is fairly difficult to extinguish. It sits there at the center of who you are, and it waits. It may have been waiting a few months, a few years, or a few decades for you to see it. But it stayed lit until you noticed. Congratulations. You noticed.

The Spark is your creativity, and you were born with it. We all were. Humans have always felt its pull. We see it in our oldest art representations—paintings on the walls in the caves at Lascaux in France from 17,000 years ago. We don't know exactly why cave paintings were made, but we guess that they were hunting maps or mythical diagrams of the constellations. One thing is certain: humans need to make things.

"Don't ask what the world needs. Ask what makes you come alive and

First we satisfied our basic needs of food, water, and shelter. Then our minds wandered to myths and God. We searched for understanding about the wonder that is existence. We made things to express how we felt. We sang. We drummed. We danced. We drew on walls and on pots with pigments made from crushed rocks. We wove grasses and made jewelry. We adorned, pierced, and tattooed. A clay pot for storing grain or hauling water from the distant spring would function equally well without adornment. But we *needed* to paint those clay pots. We *needed* to paint our bodies and our caves—to find and make meaning.

We have evidence of our creative anthropology in every museum in the world. We dream the dreams of the collective. We create so as to transform our daydreams and musings through the crucible of our own hands into an object that can reveal our awe—the miracle of this life and how we feel about it. Our souls are bound up in our hands and they always have been.

You may simply want to take a pastry class at a local bakeshop to learn how to decorate cakes with fondant, but *your desire to make things is bigger than you.* It is bigger than your daydreams. It comes from a part of you that laid on a rock and stared at the sky and wondered about why the stars shift and come back every night. It comes from our human desire to make things beautiful and meaningful—not for the sake of beauty, but because each decorative mark on that cake or that pot celebrates our existence. Each mark, each stitch, each crafted symbol etches your realness into your creations and into your life.

Your little Spark is very old. You feel its gentle tug because it pulled your great-great-great-grandmother before you. The same exact pull. We all have to do something. If not, we'd be bored. Your Spark won't go away. It's a good thing you grabbed this book so you can honor the creative life waiting for you. You're ready to take a flamenco class, learn to play the viola, paint a self-portrait, design a website, sew a quilt, bead a necklace, blow a glass vase, write that first book, join the choir, braid some hemp, design a jacket, plant a garden, or dye your own wool. Whatever it is, it will enrich and connect you. It will give your life depth. It will fill you with purpose and sparkle. It will allow you to shine your light. Let's get going.

GO DO IT.

BECAUSE WHAT THE WORLD NEEDS IS PEOPLE WHO HAVE COME ALIVE." HOWARD THURMAN

SPARK

1

Just Start

Beginning is the hardest part for many creative people. I tend to procrastinate about starting any new project. I put a whole bunch of things in my way before I start: to-do lists, errands, cleaning—it's as if I am trying to delay or defer my pleasure.

STARTING TAKES GUTS.

What if I'm terrible?
What if I fail?
What if I ruin it and waste all these materials?

You might be terrible at first. You may fail. You are definitely going to waste materials and make a mess. Then you won't. In that order.

When you are ready to begin and you feel that fear popping up, ask yourself a simple question: "What is the worst thing that might happen if I fail, make a mess, fall on my face, waste some materials, or am terrible?" Your answer might be: "I'll waste money that I don't have and I won't be able to pursue this anymore." Or, "If I mess this up, then I'll prove my parents (or spouse) right—that I'm not talented and I can't do this—and I'll be truly embarrassed."

Do This

➤ Write down the answer to your worst-case scenario question, in the present tense, right here.

➤ Next, read that sentence out loud ten times to yourself, like this:

If I fail, I will prove everyone right and I will be truly embarrassed and ashamed.
If I fail, I will prove everyone right and I will be truly embarrassed and ashamed.
If I fail, I will prove everyone right and I will be truly embarrassed and ashamed.

Getting the idea? After you have said it ten times, see how you feel. If you are still really freaked out, do it ten more times. I know this sounds crazy. You may feel strange as you do this exercise. Trust me; it works. After about the tenth time (or maybe the twentieth time), you may notice that you no longer believe your sentence or that it has less power. You may notice that it isn't true or it is extreme or you don't relate to it. The fact is that starting is scary. It brings up fears for all of us, beginners and advanced artists alike, because we are stepping into the unknown. We have to just take that first step and know that if we do make a mess of the first ten sheets of paper that we will learn a lot on the way. The more we do, the better we get, and the easier it becomes. Here are some tips to help you over the hurdle of beginning. ⟶

TIPS FOR GETTING STARTED

Don't Hoard Your Materials

I am an environmentalist, but I can tell you that being stingy with your materials, no matter what you are doing, will impede your process. If you are afraid of wasting paper, paint, clay, fabric, flour, or whatever, you will be limited in your exploration, especially at first. You've got to get in the groove. You've got to catch that wave before you can ride it.

Materials are your fishing pole, the doorway to your creativity. If you are stingy with them, you have less access to the ephemeral, magical stuff that is your own expression. Just as with fishing, you can't get too hung up about whether or not you catch the big one. You aren't after the biggest, best fish. You're just there to fish. It truly is about the process and the journey. It takes time. Getting caught up in the beauty of your trinkets is tricky business. We all want the big fish each time we sit down to our craft. But it isn't always possible. Some days your hands don't cooperate with your brain. Undoubtedly, those days are where the most growth happens. Be okay with wasting materials now and then.

Do Some Warm-Ups

Before you start any project, it helps to warm up, to stretch your muscles. If you are sitting down to write, sew, or paint, you need to get in the groove.

> Materials have their own language, pace, and rhythm—you have to tune your senses to their time frame and get into the language of your materials.

As I begin to paint, I usually get out a brush and ink. I will put the brush down and start moving it around—**not** to make a masterpiece, but to align myself with the slippery, fluid language of the ink. You can do this when quilting by stitching some loops onto scraps. My writing hero, Natalie Goldberg, advises her students to put their hand on the page and start writing. Don't stop. Keep your hand on the page and keep it moving. In this way, you tap into yourself and get in the rhythm.

Take Baby Steps

Finally, it may help you to have little tiny goals—achievable, quick steps you can take every day until you are less intimidated by starting. You can almost avoid the big moment of starting entirely if you keep your work out and step into it a little bit every day; then it is more like doing a puzzle that's sitting on the dining table—you just do a bit here and there. That way you aren't starting but rather continuing a conversation you've already begun.

SPARK 2

Create the Space

ARIZONA ARTIST CYNDI COON STORES MOUNTAINS OF MATERIALS FOR ART JOURNALING, PAINTING, AND CRAFTING ON FLOOR-TO-CEILING SHELVES. EACH BIN IS CLEARLY MARKED SO SHE KNOWS WHAT'S INSIDE.

You need a space, big or small, in which to be creative. Having a good work space cements you to your dreams. The creative space is a launchpad, refuge, retreat, temple, labyrinth, and safety net. It gives you a sense of purpose. Your space is a flagpole on the moon. If you believe in your dream enough to make a spot for it in your life and mark it with a flag, then you're more likely to pursue your passion and hear the Spark when it calls.

Even if you're still figuring out your creative direction, there's an obstacle in the way if you're always having to move everyone else's stuff out of the way before you start. The Spark might not stick around for two hours of housekeeping. It helps to have space ready. For some, a sewing room might be a cleared-off dining table, with other materials hiding in a nearby cabinet or closet, or it might be an armchair for knitting. For others, a separate messy space might be necessary. It isn't always possible to have a separate room, but creating a space with boundaries is important, regardless.

If you're a baker, you may just need a bit of kitchen space, but how do you claim that space as yours and separate from your family's? Create a special place (a drawer or cupboard) for all your stuff—tools, pans, books. Claim it as your own and don't let it get mixed in with the daily flotsam of life. Own it. Mark it. Protect it. In this way you advocate for yourself, your pursuits, and your special creative time.

One way to claim your space is by making it beautiful. Surround yourself with beauty. It will beckon you.

Surround yourself with beauty. It will beckon you.

SEWING PATTERN DESIGNER SHELLY FIGUEROA OF FIGGY'S PATTERNS CREATED THIS LOVELY NOOK BY THE WINDOW IN HER ATTIC STUDIO. LET YOUR STUDIO HAVE BEAUTIFUL MOMENTS THAT CALL YOU TO SIT AND JUST BE.

CREATIVE CHAOS

When I work, a tornado quickly brews in my studio—papers, fabrics, and trash go flying in all directions. By the time I am done, my 300-square-foot studio is unrecognizable. The surfaces and floor are covered in detritus and remnants. Because I know this about myself, I want my materials behind closed cabinet doors so the room feels calm. I know I'm going to make a mess as I work, and it would feel too chaotic for me if my materials were showing. This is personal preference. I have other friends who like to see their materials so they can be inspired by them.

Store materials so you can get into the flow easily, so your tools are ready when you are. Organize your space in a way that suits your particular needs.

CLUTTER

Clutter doesn't help. Even if your space is periodically messy, you don't want it to be cluttered. It can't be a space that you share with your kids' soccer gear, unfolded laundry, and last year's Christmas ornaments. You deserve better than that. I highly encourage you to take charge here. Put your foot down. Make space for yourself. Find a home for the other junk and don't let it migrate back.

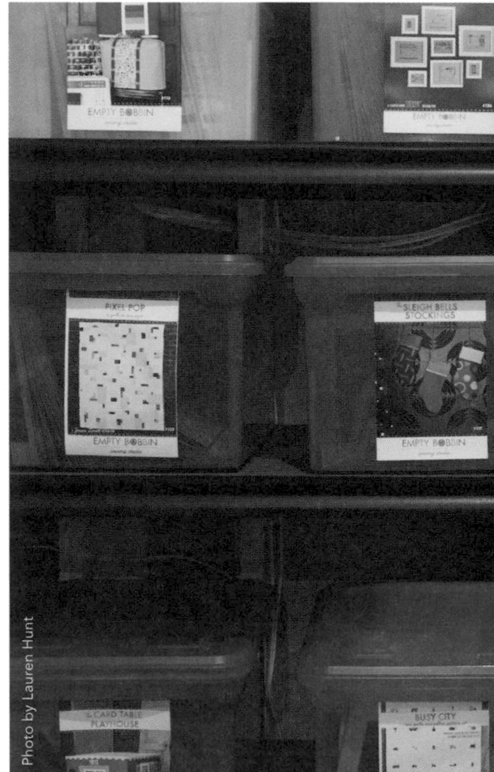

Photo by Lauren Hunt

MODERN QUILTER AND PATTERN DESIGNER SHEA HENDERSON OF EMPTY BOBBIN SEWING STUDIO IN KANSAS CITY, MISSOURI, COLOR-CODED HER STORAGE BINS.

BINS

I have never met a studio that didn't rely on bins. IKEA, Target, and organization stores have bins. You will need them. Shoe boxes work well too. When organizing any space, put like with like: all acrylic paints together, all sandpaper together, all drawing pencils together. Depending on how compulsive you are, you may want to label the bins clearly from the outside so you don't have to peek inside to see what's there. Color-coding your bins is a really pretty way to keep things organized.

IN MY 300-SQUARE-FOOT STUDIO, I MAXIMIZE COUNTER SPACE AND HIDE ALL THE MATERIALS IN CABINETS TO CREATE A VISUALLY CALM SPACE.

COUNTER OR TABLE SPACE

You will likely need empty, unimpeded counter or table space for working and spreading out. Be mindful when planning. If space allows, get more tables and counters than you think you need. You will need many horizontal surfaces for storing works in progress, as well as other surfaces for creating.

Consider Your Needs and Requirements

- Do you keep your space messy or tidy, organized or chaotic? Do you need lots of cabinets, drawers, boxes, or bins?

- Do you need fresh air from an open window? Special ventilation for toxic materials?

- Do you like to work on the floor? On a desk? At an easel? Standing up?

- What else do you need? A computer? A sewing machine? A pottery wheel? A sink? Write down your specific needs here so you can have a plan when you start to create your space.

In college, I worked for a famous artist named Kiki Smith. She shows in museums and galleries all over the world. She remains one of my all-time favorite artists. Her vision of the world, rendered through powerful images of the body and the animal world, tells a resonant story. Kiki had a studio that took up a few floors of a building in Manhattan. But the work she does in her studio is just a sliver of her total work. Her creativity is always on, and it goes with her. We would run errands, and she would be knitting the whole time. She made art everywhere—in taxicabs, on the phone, at artist residency programs. Her hands were always moving. Take your studio with you. Create an awesome space for yourself, but make things everywhere!

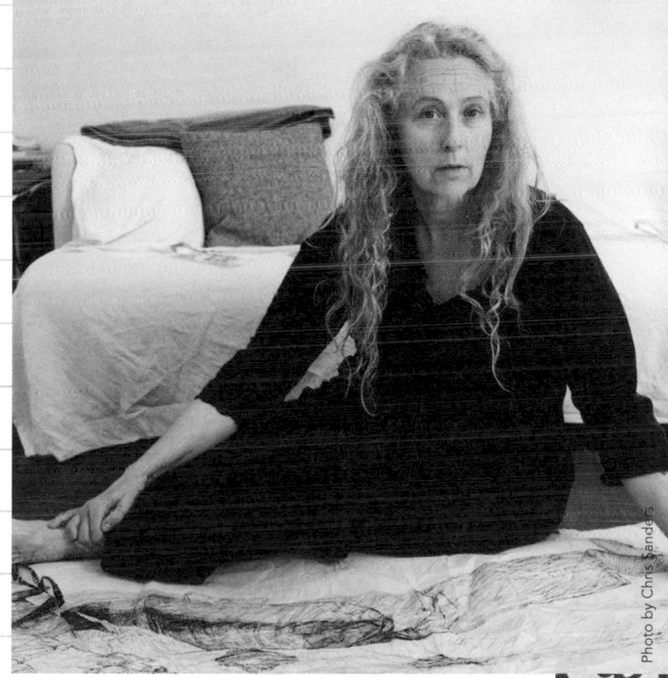

Photo by Chris Sanders

KIKI SMITH

SPARK 3

Take a Class

JAIME JENNINGS AND AMBER CORCORAN OWN FANCY TIGER CRAFTS, A RETAIL CRAFT AND CLASS SHOP IN DENVER, COLORADO. THEY HAVE HOSTED AN OPEN CRAFT NIGHT EVERY TUESDAY NIGHT FOR SEVEN YEARS. "BEING IN THIS COMMUNITY IS ONE OF OUR TOP REASONS FOR DOING WHAT WE DO, AND IT DRIVES OUR LOVE OF OUR CRAFTS," SAYS JAIME.

Photo by Amber Corcoran

The main thing I hear from people about what keeps them from their creative dreams is: "But I didn't go to school for that." This lack of training can make people feel paralyzed. While an education is not the only route to achieving your dreams, studying something definitely has its perks. You get an amazing energy and buzz from taking a class. You learn about technique, craft, and process—the bones of a working practice. You get tips from others in the field about integrating that practice into your life. You develop a vocabulary and learn how to see and discuss what you make (critique).

Formal training instills in you a sense of confidence. Confidence comes from gaining fluency. Classes will help you feel comfortable exploring your creativity. When you start something new, you are not expected to be good. You just need to have an open heart and be gentle with yourself as you learn.

If you are like me, you may feel *frexcited* when you think about showing up at your first class. Frexcited is that special mixture of frightened and excited—tingling shoulders and goose bumps, silly grinning, and butterflies in your stomach. If you have any of those sensations, then you are off to a good start! If you feel propelled to open the door and at the same time want to run and hide, that is also a good start. Just trust.

LOCAL CLASSES

Start researching classes and programs at schools in your area. Use Google or Yelp (or a similar search tool) to search "sewing classes" or "adult modern dance classes" or whatever it is you are interested in. You may be surprised how many great results you will get. If you don't even know what class you want to take, see my list of possibilities (page 19).

Local shops and studios are a great option for beginning. If you get more serious, you can move on to more formal study and training at a local community college or university if you feel you need to.

Photo by Tracey Freeman

SEWING PATTERN DESIGNER SHELLY FIGUEROA HAS TAUGHT HUNDREDS OF KIDS HOW TO SEW IN HER LOVELY LAKE OSWEGO, OREGON, ATTIC SPACE.

When you start your class, soak it all up. Ask lots of questions—and not just of the teacher. Ask your fellow students about what works for them: which local stores sell the best materials, which online retailers and suppliers they like. Your fellow students may teach you as much as your teacher. They will be supercharged and excited just like you. The kindred spirits you meet in your classes will give you a way of connecting to your new craft. Sharing people's stories while learning a new craft feels wonderful.

ONLINE LEARNING

What if you don't have any good options for classes in your town? Luckily, online learning has exploded in recent years and there are incredible sites for learning almost anything from home. I have taken online classes to learn everything from sewing a caftan to using Adobe Illustrator 101. Additionally, there are many free tutorials on YouTube, and many bloggers post relevant free downloadable tutorials. Start digging around online and you will find many resources.

Some of my favorites:

beaducation.com offers free (and for-fee) jewelry classes.

ceramicartsdaily.org offers an extensive forum and DVDs about pottery and clay.

craftsy.com offers classes on everything from quilting, sewing, and embroidery to paper, fine art, knitting, spinning, cake decorating, and jewelry.

creativebug.com is an amazing online crafting site. You can learn how to make your own lip balm, a beeswax collage on canvas, or a leather wrap bracelet. The site creates lovely tutorials in the studios of savvy professionals in the crafting/design world.

ctpub.com is a great resource for books, DVDs, and other products related to quilting, surface design, sewing, fiber and needle arts, and mixed media.

escoffieronline.com, the website of the renowned culinary academy Escoffier International, offers online cooking and pastry programs.

interweavestore.com offers many DVDs and resources for beading, knitting, quilting, jewelry, mixed media, weaving, spinning, and sewing.

kingarthurflour.com offers wonderful free baking classes online.

lillarogers.com is the site of a leading art licensing agent who teaches online classes on making art that sells.

marthastewart.com is the website of my all-time favorite crafty superhero. Her site is full of amazing, elegant tutorials and inspiration for the budding (or experienced) crafter.

moma.org offers self-guided or teacher-led courses about the history and techniques of modern art.

nicolesclasses.com is a wonderful resource for photography classes, flower arranging classes, graphic design classes for Illustrator and Photoshop, and even watercolor classes.

online.berklee.edu offers great music classes from the famed Berklee College of Music.

ravelry.com is an online forum for knitting and crochet.

skillshare.com offers classes in design, fashion, film, food, music, photography, writing, and technology.

welding-courses.net teaches you welding skills online!

writingclasses.com offers many online writing classes from Gotham Writer's Workshop in New York City.

OFF YOU GO.

Do This

➤ Go Google a class and get going! Make a list of your local and online options right here and sign up:

SPARK
4

The Crazies

Blah. Blah. Blah.

IT ALL STARTS WITH THAT TINY SPARK.

And then come the Crazies.

The Crazies are the opposite of the Spark. They are the voices that tell you that your urge to follow your creative dream is crazy. They say, "Hogwash! Nonsense! What is wrong with you? You have such a nice life—why are you dissatisfied?" The Crazies are programmed to trip you up. They represent all the people who ever told you that you couldn't. You've heard these voices your entire life from the dream stealers of Responsibility, Security, Financial Plans, 401(k)s, Your Parents' Fears, and our culture's weird value system and mythologized/misunderstood creative life that goes like this:

> We love art. We need art.
>
> We love creative people, but we don't like to pay too much for what they create.
>
> If you choose a creative life, you choose a life of poverty, lack, and struggle. You will suffer for your art.
> (Which isn't really true.)

They inhabit your mind and churn out a bunch of nonsense to keep you in the place where you behave "rationally and responsibly." The Crazies love that—the things that make you "normal" and "acceptable," the things that make you "blend in."

The Crazies inhabit all of us. I'm a lifelong artist, abstract painter, and designer, and I trained at one of the finest of art schools (Rhode Island School of Design). Yet I still run into the Crazies. But you can hush them up. Here's how: →

Do This

Let Go

- First, let go of the voices that say you can't. It might be your own voice or the voices of others saying your creative desire is folly and it will certainly never bring you money, so why would you even try? Blah, blah, blah … the Crazies drone on. They can be very persuasive.
- Let go of the part of you that actually believes those voices—the part that believes you can't:

INSERT YOUR CREATIVE DESIRE HERE: PLAY GUITAR, PAINT, BAKE, DANCE, DESIGN, WHATEVER IT IS.

- Let go of the part of you that says you're a fraud, a faker, no good, untalented, incapable, unchangeable, too old, too poor, too rusty, too busy, too tired, too scheduled, too overworked, too stressed, whatever it is—let it go.

THE PART OF YOU THAT ACTUALLY BELIEVES THOSE VOICES DOESN'T SERVE YOU.

That part of you is:	But quickly it becomes:
CRITIC	BUZZKILL • AXMAN
EDITOR	MURDERER OF DREAMS
JUDGE	PARALYZER • **BULLY**

Life generally tampers with creativity because being a grown-up requires a great deal of organization and management. While being a grown-up is necessary, it often comes at the expense of the messier and certainly harder-to-define urges of the human heart. One of those urges is the desire to create something—not for any specific reason, not for financial gain, not for ego gratification, but just because it feels good.

Play

We all need to be more like young kids—to play, to run around in the backyard of our souls until the sun sets and then keep playing until we're called in for dinner. Even though you need to pay bills and upgrade the dishwasher, just for now, as you read this book, try to play as much as possible. **IF SOMETHING FEELS FUN, KEEP DOING IT.**

Notice

Tune in to yourself to get rid of the Crazies. Be aware of the voices as they pop up. Notice them. Don't judge them. Just notice if you hear them and maybe write down what they say on slips of paper … "I can't." … "I don't have enough time." …

Box Them Up

Grab a container with a lid and put the slips of paper in it. This allows you to acknowledge your own self-limiting negative messages while choosing to contain them so they don't get in your way. Over time, after successful creative sessions, you can open up the container and tear a piece off a slip of paper. Throw that away and put the rest of the slip back. Slowly, the Crazies will diminish and you will remove them from your life.

Escort Them to the Door

Tell your inner critic to take some time off. Tell your inner planner that what you are doing won't ruin your retirement plans. When you arrive at that distant shore, you'll get there with an intact psyche and a heart full of passion, ready to go throw clay pots in your garage, write your memoir, or make beachside watercolor paintings. Tell your inner naysayer—that voice that tells you that you probably won't be good, and you already aren't good enough—to buzz off.

SPARK

5

Time

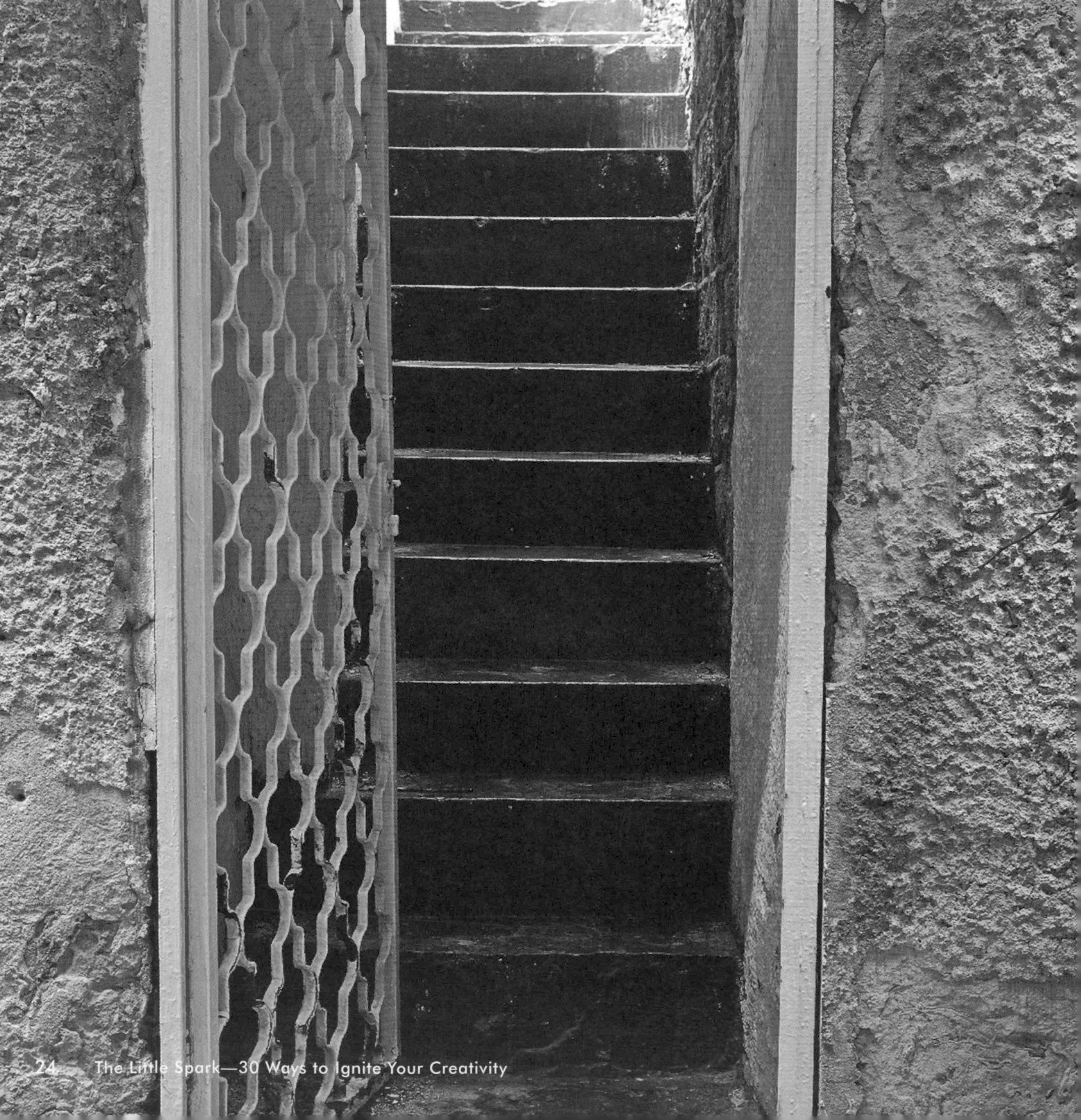

SPARK 5

"Forever is composed of nows."
EMILY DICKINSON

It is a fact of modern life that we are busy. Cultivating a creative life will require some thoughtful shuffling of things to make room for it. Be aware of your own rhythms as you establish a creative practice so you can take the path of least resistance (which is always the right path). I don't believe in the "struggling artist" paradigm.

IF I AM STRUGGLING AT ANYTHING, I GENERALLY FEEL LIKE I NEED TO FIND A BETTER WAY.

IF DOORS ARE OPENING BY THEMSELVES, THEN I KNOW I'M ON THE RIGHT TRACK.

Pay attention to the little things in your life that are like green lights telling you to go.

Do This

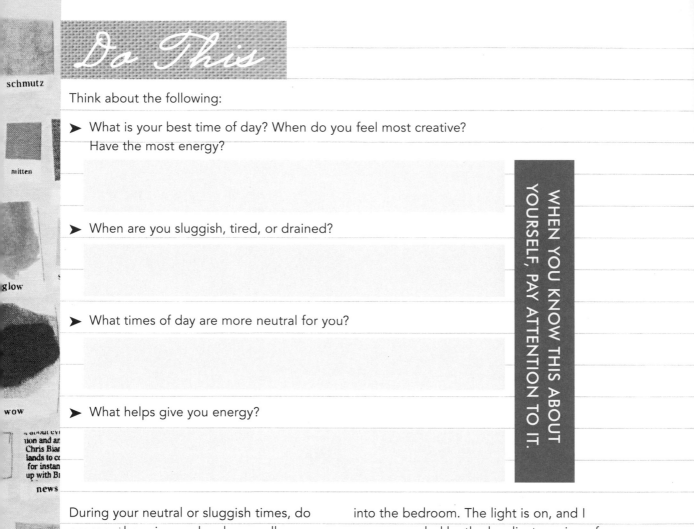

Think about the following:

- What is your best time of day? When do you feel most creative? Have the most energy?

- When are you sluggish, tired, or drained?

- What times of day are more neutral for you?

- What helps give you energy?

WHEN YOU KNOW THIS ABOUT YOURSELF, PAY ATTENTION TO IT.

During your neutral or sluggish times, do grocery shopping, make phone calls, or clean the house. Get work and obligations done when you have energy. When you have one of those sacred hours free during your creative time, reserve it—be available for your Spark.

As I write this chapter, it is 2:15 a.m. I have been writing since the Spark woke me at 1:00 a.m. Nothing in me wanted to heed its call. I had no paper, pen, laptop, or iPhone near my bed. But after a few moments, I stumbled through the dark house and found an old 7B art pencil and a spiral-bound notebook and started writing. Over the past hour, kids and the dog have wandered into the bedroom. The light is on, and I am surrounded by the loveliest purring of their collective breathing. I turned the air-conditioning way down, and I am having fun scrawling this chapter with my art pencil. I am not a night owl. I like to sleep. But when the Spark popped up, so did I. I let myself be available for it because I know it is precious inspiration. Certainly, I wouldn't remember more than three bullet points by tomorrow morning if I didn't write anything down, so I had to tune in and not miss the opportunity.

I have many friends who sew and quilt after they put their children to sleep. I get too amped up if I work at night. It makes it hard for me to calm down and fall asleep.

My creative hours are between 10 a.m. and 4 p.m. I dawdle until 11 a.m. I find it helpful to mess around sometimes—do busywork and errands until I can feel my internal rhythms shift, and I know it is time to get into the studio. Sometimes, I'm not quite ready, but I still go in and start doing something—even if it's just replying to business emails.

I know of a local painter who has young children. He also has a day job. The only time he could find to paint was at 4:30 a.m. To squeeze the most out of his creative life, he found a way to squeeze it *into* his life. No doubt, this takes dedication, persistence, and sacrifice. We have to tune in to our own lives to locate those precious creative hours.

Ask yourself this question: **What am I willing to move out of the way to make room for my joy, ecstasy, and passion?**

I claw my way to what's important to me. I have the same piles of laundry as you. I want to be a deeply connected and present mother to my kids, just like you. I want to go on date night to Vietnamese food with my husband, just like you. I want to exercise, just like you. There isn't any time left for your Spark, right? You think, "How will I possibly squeeze in one more thing?" You will. There is time. Things can shift and move. Be flexible and creative. Find some grace (page 40) and you'll find the time.

For one day, don't clean your house. Don't reply to emails. Don't go to the grocery store. Not *every* day—just today. Let go of your "shoulds." Your house won't fall into ruin if you do this periodically, but it will give you few extra hours here and there.

Do This

- You may not realize how much time you spend doing stuff you don't really have to do—such as reading your social media feeds or watching TV. What behaviors or patterns could you let go of to find more time for your passion?

- Schedule your creative time. Put it on the calendar. Set an alarm on your phone. Be prepared—have everything you need so you can dive right in.

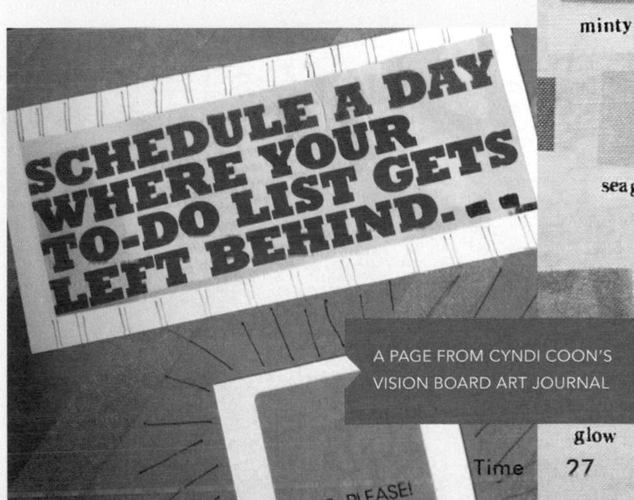

SCHEDULE A DAY WHERE YOUR TO-DO LIST GETS LEFT BEHIND.
YES, PLEASE!

A PAGE FROM CYNDI COON'S VISION BOARD ART JOURNAL

SPARK

6

Make a Huge Mess

Every day when I pick up my daughter from preschool she is covered in remnants of her creative day, and I mean *covered*. She is dirty, sandy, gritty, painted, and stained. There's sandwich on her face and sand in her pockets. Her shins are unrecognizably brownish-gray. I kneel down next to her, beaming, and say, "That's what I like to see! I know you had a good day because you got messy!"

Do you honestly think I want that dirty child in my new car? *Absolutely not!* But I know I am being a really good mom in those moments because I am encouraging her creativity and validating her process and exploration. She can get in the bath later. Life is filled with opportunities, and if you are worried about getting dirty or making a mess, either metaphorically or for real, then you will be limited in your possibilities.

And so it is with grown-ups. You know you are on the right track if you are making a mess of something. You have to fall on your face sometimes. Who is your life for? Is it a big performance that you have rigged up with hidden strings and edited with Instagram-style filters to make you seem beautiful and perfect all the time? I did that for a long time. The years I Photoshopped my life into perfection and managed my image for some perceived gaze were some of the least creative of my life.

This isn't a show.

PERFECTIONISM IS THE ENEMY OF THE CREATIVE ACT.

It constricts you and confines you. It squeezes you into unrecognizable, contorted shapes. Believe me. I know. I did it. I white-knuckled my life, art, and relationships, thinking that if I could control the outcome, and not get sandwich on my face, then everyone would know that I was doing it *right* and that I was good enough. Thankfully, I got over that.

When Allen Ginsberg wrote his epic poem, *Howl*, he set out to write a poem he would never show to anyone. Look what happened. Freedom from perceived judgment can be liberating—the freedom to be raw, honest, gritty, sandy, messy, and truthful.

You are okay and good enough exactly as you are, whether you are amazing at your craft or not. It doesn't have to be tidy. It doesn't have to look perfect. But it does have to be true to you.

When you dig around in yourself, you may find some bits that aren't pretty. You may find some smears, some tears, some pain, some unresolved grief. That stuff makes you *you*. Let your life be your laboratory—the pretty, the ugly, the tender, the vulnerable, the honest. All the parts of you may surface at some point. That is the healing gift of making things.

> Allowing the messy part of the self—the unresolved part—to have a voice is a way of healing and a way of understanding yourself and the world.

In her book *Wild Mind: Living the Writer's Life*, Natalie Goldberg sums this idea up eloquently: "So finally a writer must be willing to sit at the bottom of the pit, commit herself to stay there, and let all the wild animals approach, even call them up, then face them, write them down, and not run away."

Creativity most definitely has its perks—it can reveal our truest selves to us. Cracks of light open up in our hearts so we can shine.

Today, make a mess. Take off the Photoshopped filters you wear over your life. Sing in your car with the windows down because it feels good. Sit down with the intention of making a mess, of making something you may or may not show anyone.

➤ Here is an optional exercise. You can do this here in this book or on a piece of paper that you can shred afterward. Write down a few sandy, gritty details of your life. Write down three painful memories that you are afraid may bubble up as you're going about your creative life.

Honor them as beautiful, tender parts of yourself. Know that you are not perfect and that no one is. Know that the messiness that is your humanness connects you to others. The more able you are to share your truth in your creativity, the more whole you will become, and the more people can connect to your story.

Photo by Howard Jones

"Perfectionism is the voice of the oppressor, the enemy of the people. It will keep you cramped and insane your whole life... Perfectionism is a mean, frozen form of idealism, while messes are the artist's true friend." ANNE LAMOTT

SPARK

7

Permission

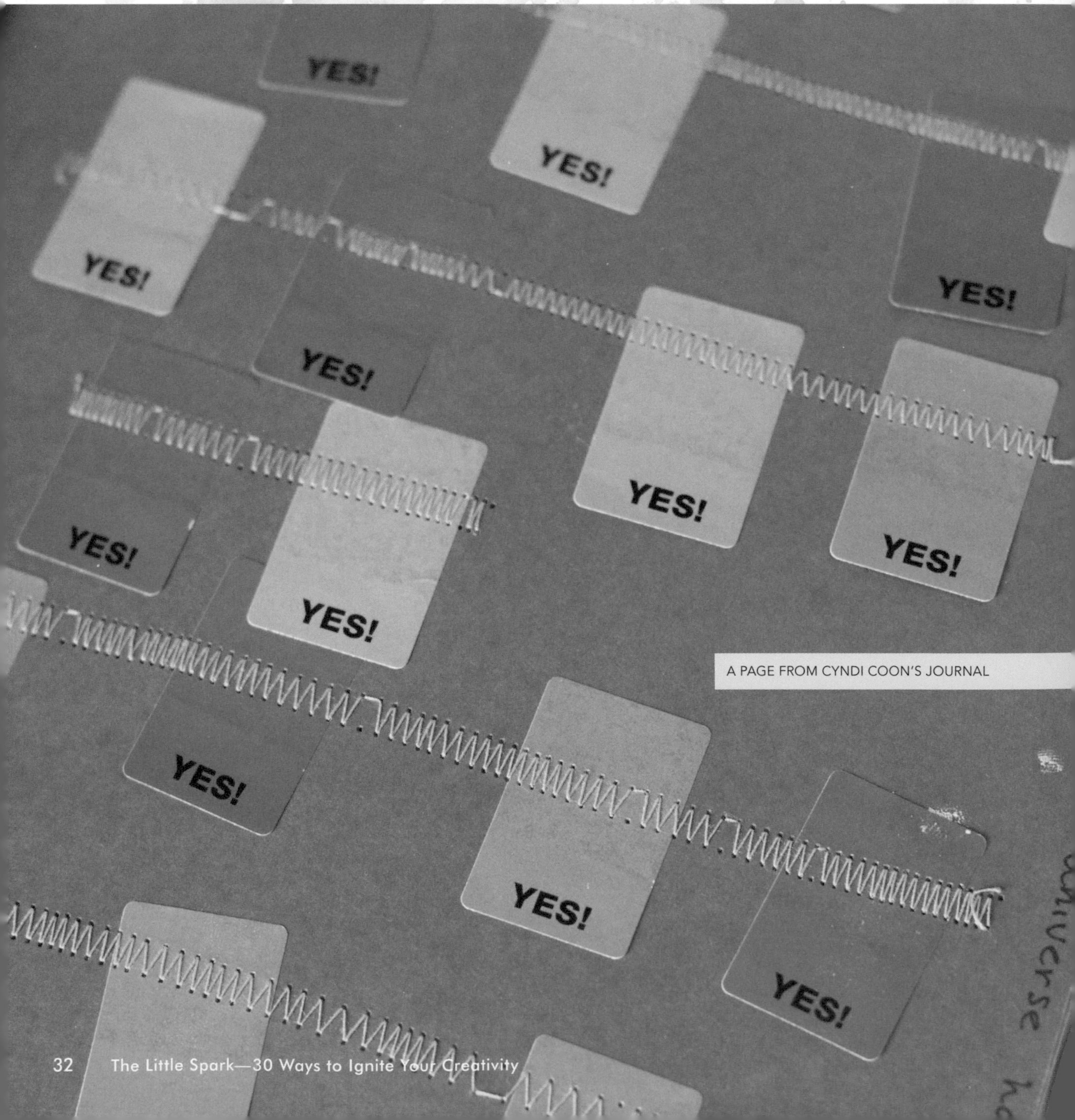

A PAGE FROM CYNDI COON'S JOURNAL

First, my creative parents said yes to my creativity, even as a baby. Then my first real art teacher was Dicki Arn. Starting in kindergarten, she held my Spark in her palms and blew gently on my tiny flame all the way until sixth grade. We are now Facebook friends. In my heart, I know she is the reason my whole life has unfolded as it has.

"The best teachers are those who show you where to look, but don't tell you what to see."

ALEXANDRA K. TRENFOR

As I grew up, I studied with several teachers, and eventually I met Anne Arrasmith, an artist and visionary working in downtown Birmingham, Alabama, at a studio she created called Space One Eleven. I was probably about eleven when I started studying with Anne. I studied with her until college. Her teaching style was radical—she didn't teach anything. She just said to her students, "Come on in, y'all. Now, let's get to work!"

She gave her students nothing but space, time, materials, and permission. She offered an open door to her wild studio filled with crazy, sophisticated materials and tools. Space One Eleven took up a whole old building downtown. It had a wood shop and rooms upon rooms of stuff—it housed a pottery studio, a resident intern who painted huge oil paintings of weird Grateful Dead–inspired frogs, and a photographer's lab.

She would look at us, mere children, and ask, "What do you want to make today?" as if we knew. She assumed we did. And we did.

> She trusted us to know what we wanted to make.
> She didn't give us assignments, lectures, or instructions.
> She gave us possibility and permission.

Her gift fueled my passion and creativity. In Anne's studio, everything was possible. She taught us to trust our own urges and creative voices; she helped us heed the little Spark. We'd start with an idea, and she'd walk us around the studio showing us ways that we could achieve that vision, pointing us to mixed-media materials that real artists used—not Play-Doh and construction paper, but airplane glue and crumpled paper with gesso.

Photo by Beau Gustafson

SPACE ONE ELEVEN COFOUNDERS ANNE ARRASMITH AND PETER PRINZ

It is important to remember and be mindful of the blessings and resources in our lives that allow us freedom—open doors, yesses, possibility. In other chapters you have detailed things that have interfered with the little Spark over your life, but now you get to write down your blessings. You're lucky to have enough money to buy a book on creativity, right? And the tools and classes? The time and space? These are your gifts. When you see them and live from that place of gratitude, it helps you move further in the direction of abundant creativity. For me, there is nothing more grounding than gratitude. If you are grateful, it means you're connected to your blessings, your source, your gifts. You can act from that joy.

Do This

- Go find people who share your passions or interests and hang out, get a coffee, and chat. When we feel supported and connected, it connects us more deeply to our path.

SEEK OUT PEOPLE WHO SAY YES. SEEK OUT PEOPLE WHO GIVE YOU PERMISSION, WHETHER TEACHERS OR FRIENDS.

- Interview your creative friends and crafty role models. Some people are **book people** and some people are **people people**. I am a people person. My husband is a book person. So, when we are faced with a problem or question, I am likely to find someone to ask, and he is likely to consult a research article. Which type are you? If you are a book person, you might want to rely on Google searches to help you navigate in your quest for examples of a creative role model. Spend time in the library looking up people in your chosen field.

  If you are like me, and you prefer to chat, call up a friend or acquaintance you know to be a creative person living a creative life and ask if you can buy her a coffee. Pick her brain about her creative life. What works for her? What doesn't? Any helpful tips, hints, or tricks? Ask tons of questions, and most especially the questions you are afraid, nervous, or too embarrassed to ask. Your friend will most likely love helping you and feel flattered that you chose her to ask. Remember, we all like to talk about ourselves. This most likely won't be a nuisance to your acquaintance; she will be happy to share.

Count Your Blessings

➤ What are the blessings in your life that enable your creativity? Resources? Experiences? I hope you need extra paper for this! I hope you need a whole journal, but start right here, right now.

➤ Who are your open doors? Teachers? Friends? Write down who or what helps enable your passion and creativity, who has given you permission:

"Surround yourself with the dreamers and the doers, the believers and thinkers, but most of all, surround yourself with those who see greatness within you, even when you don't see it yourself." EDMUND LEE

SPARK

8

Process

AYUMI TAKAHASHI IS A SUPERSTAR BLOGGER, MODERN QUILTER, AND DESIGNER LIVING IN JAPAN. HER STUDIO AND PROCESS REFLECT THE SMALLER SCALE OF JAPANESE HOMES. ORGANIZATION IS A MUST IN A SMALL SPACE. AYUMI'S FUNKY, FRESH SENSIBILITY IS MIRRORED IN HER STUDIO. INSPIRING PROJECTS AND PATCHWORK HANG ON THE WALLS.

Photo by Ayumi Takahashi

Each day is a microcosm of the larger picture of your life. Each moment you spend tending to the Spark, the more your life will go in that direction. As your working process evolves, begin to notice it so you understand what helps you as you work.

After a while, you will learn how to incorporate the creative process into your days—how to integrate your dream into your reality. The more energy you spend on your passion, and the more your creative passion reveals itself to you, the more it will grow.

"How we spend our days is, of course, how we spend our lives."

ANNIE DILLARD

REMEMBER:

HOW YOU DO ANYTHING IS HOW YOU DO EVERYTHING.

That means that your essential nature is revealed through whatever activity you're doing. If you are filled with contentment and peace as you do your work, then you are stepping into a life of contentment and peace. Conversely, if you are frustrated and rushing to get to the next part of your day, then you are creating a life of hurry and frustration.

GETTIN' READY TO GET READY

My awesome little brother, Adam, owns a big, successful credit card processing company in Atlanta. He is pretty much the exact opposite of me. Where he is straight, I am crooked. Where he is black-and-white, I'm the Pantone deck of colors. He advised me as I was starting my newest business, and in his characteristic terse, Southern-gentleman style he would commonly interrupt my ramblings with, "Um, Carrie, you're just gettin' ready to get ready." It drove me crazy. He was always dismissing all my concerns with that one little sentence—until I *got* it.

His point was that we (small business owners and creative people) don't often pay attention to the right things. His main question was, "What are you doing to make money for your business today?" Everything else is just shuffling papers, and messing around on social media, and blustering on about which printer to use. That's all just "gettin' ready to get ready"—it is the nonsense we do that keeps us busy and makes us feel productive.

> But what feels productive doesn't necessarily move you toward your goal.

In your creative life you will find that you have your own process. It is as unique as you are. And most likely at least half of it will be "gettin' ready to get ready." Over time you'll begin to see patterns in your process. For me, I can see cleaning, sweeping, and organizing as absolutely crucial to my creative process, but I only do that stuff when I am *not* creating. It is the dark side of my moon. It is the mundane work of the creative life, yet I value it. I have developed a certain dance. When it is time to carve some space in my studio and clear stuff away, it is almost a ritual, a metaphor for starting fresh.

SOLO VS. WINGMAN

You will notice as you get into your process that you are likely to fall into one of two camps. The first type wants to do everything alone. People in the second category want a wingman, a friend, to join them on their adventure or work with them. You will learn which type you are fairly quickly. I am usually a solo flyer. My mom likes a wingman. Figure it out and act accordingly. Neither is right or wrong.

BECAUSE MY MOM LIKES A WINGMAN, I HAVE DONE A LOT OF COOL WORKSHOPS IN MY LIFE.

THE WORK IS THE REWARD

Procrastination, busywork, boredom, deadlines—these are all part of the creative life. Get to know them. It isn't fireworks and butterflies all the time. You'll develop your own methods and style as you work more and more. Ease into the work. The work is what you're after. It is the jewel of the journey—not the objects you create, but the work itself, the act of creating.

DEADLINES

Take note of what works for you and what doesn't. For example, I respond very well to the heat of the pressure imposed on me by a firm deadline. Many creative people thrive under the pressure of a deadline. I like it when I am accountable to other people for getting things done in a certain time frame. Otherwise, I can sometimes dawdle. My husband, conversely, is incredible about measuring his work into manageable increments and being diligent over the course of months to achieve that same end. We are all different. Accept your nature and work with what you've got.

Just before a deadline I go into the cave of my work. The spirit and intensity of the work engulfs everything and blots out the sun, my friends—everything except family. I stay in my cave until the project is done. Then I wander out of the studio, blinking into the sunlight, and I rejoin the world.

Work as much as you can. Period. Be as mindful as you can about your process. Get to know it so you can honor its rhythms.

> "Don't compare your beginning to someone else's middle."
>
> JON ACUFF

PATIENCE

Rome wasn't built in a day. Don't get discouraged. Be patient with the process. Exploring the creative journey is often more valuable than the creative product itself. The fishing is what it's about; the fish is a lucky by-product and the excuse to make things. But enjoy the process free from chasing expectations. Be gentle as you find your voice and your wings.

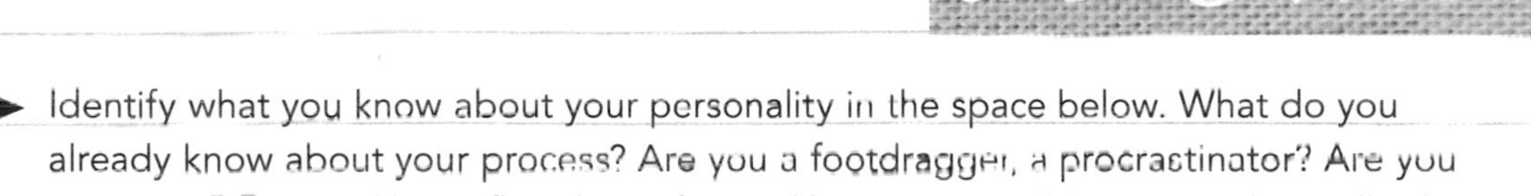

➤ Identify what you know about your personality in the space below. What do you already know about your process? Are you a footdragger, a procrastinator? Are you tenacious? Do you like to fly solo or do you like a wingman? Is your work usually slow and steady or pants on fire? How do you respond to deadlines?

SPARK

9

Grace

SUSAN SILVERMAN HAS DANCED HER WHOLE LIFE. SHE TEACHES AND OWNS A SMALL STUDIO IN PHOENIX, ARIZONA, CALLED DANCE THEATER WEST. SHE IS FILLED WITH GRACE. SHE'S IN IT FOR THE LOVE. GRACE IS THE HINGE BETWEEN EFFORT AND EFFORTLESS, AND IN THIS IMAGE YOU CAN SEE HER AT THAT EXACT MOMENT.

Grace comes from within; it is the hinge between effort and effortless.

We are programmed to think that work has to be hard to be valuable—that we are supposed to struggle in order to yield the most prized outcome. Nothing could be further from the truth. In fact, I would say that the opposite is true. Work can often be easy. Taking the path of least resistance will serve you. Doors swing wide on their hinges when we move from the heart. Creativity is a flowing thing. You can't white-knuckle it into existence. Loosen your grip and give it some space to flow.

In yoga there is a name for this, from the very old yoga sutras of Patanjali (Yoga Sutra 2, "Sadhana Pada")—*Sthira Sukham Asanam* is Sanskrit for "balancing ease and grace with work and effort." This is absolutely critical for a creative practice. If we are only full of effort and we are trying to muscle and power our way through our work, our yoga, our project, then it will seem harder than it should. We might feel tense or uptight as we work.

AND HERE WE ARE, SUSIE'S STUDENTS, EASING INTO OUR MOVEMENTS. LEARNING TO FEEL FLUID IN OUR SKIN. LISTENING TO THE SPARK.

We are too forceful and lose the grace and flow. Conversely, if we are too relaxed and not putting in enough effort, then we might be sloppy, lackadaisical, careless, or lazy. Grace comes from not only being filled with purposefulness and spirit as we work, but also enjoying the moment and being present with the process. Grace is the hinge between effort and effortless. There is a moment in our creative flow in which we are utterly absorbed, content, focused, and present with the moment and everything in it. For me, this is what it is all about. This is what keeps us coming back for more—that limitless feeling of being in our own flow. It feels liberated and liberating. It is the power of creating something with our own hands. My favorite quote comes from Mother Teresa: "We cannot do great things on this Earth, only small things with great love." That moment between effort and effortless is filled with great love.

A wise woman in Big Sur, California, Jan McCool, helped me understand this. I told her that I was afraid to design my first line of fabric (and write my first book) because everyone I spoke to said it was hard when they did it. She looked at me, with her water-clear blue eyes, and said, "That's their story—their experience: Each time someone tells you her story, you put it on and wear it like a coat. Many of those coats don't fit you and yet you are wearing them. Why are you wearing everyone else's coat? Take off their coats. Give them back. What does your coat look like? Your story is yours. It may be completely different from theirs. Your story may be that writing a book is easy and designing your fabric is easy." Guess what? She was right. If you step into that place of grace, you act in a way that seeks balance. I now consciously choose to not be stressed, to not feel split between parenting and work, to not freak out.

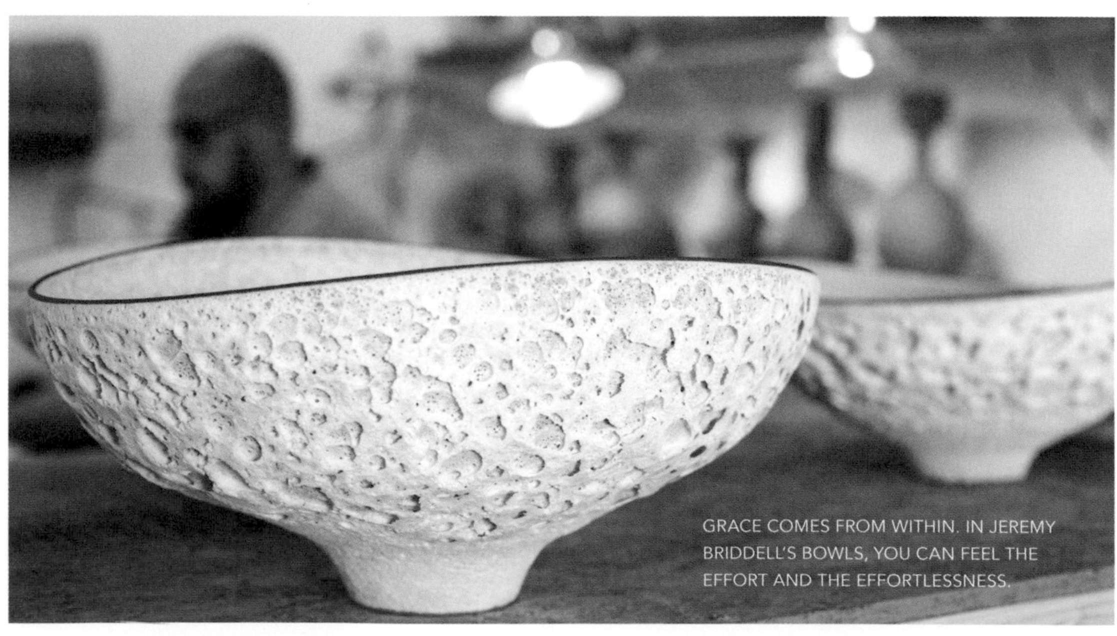
GRACE COMES FROM WITHIN. IN JEREMY BRIDDELL'S BOWLS, YOU CAN FEEL THE EFFORT AND THE EFFORTLESSNESS.

- Can you identify the coats your parents gave you? Or your friends? Are you still wearing them right now? Wearing their stories instead of your own? Write down in detail what your own unique coat looks like. What is it made of? Is it heavy or light? What color is it? Is it made of gold? Is it made of light?

- After you write, if you find that you are wearing a bunch of other people's coats, give them back. Close your eyes and picture the people who shared their stories with you. Thank them for sharing their experiences with you. Tell them that you no longer need their stories. Hand their coats back to them.

  Write intentions to fill your process with grace or whatever it is that you want for yourself.

Break Your Own Rules

I PROBABLY WROTE HALF OF THIS BOOK UP IN THE TREE FORT WE MADE (ALTHOUGH I WASN'T USUALLY IN MY SUPER-CUTE TOMS WEDGE HIGH HEELS). IT FELT RIGHT TO SHAKE IT UP AND BE CREATIVE ABOUT MY WRITING LOCATIONS, TO PICK CREATIVE SPOTS. I WROTE ONE CHAPTER IN MY DAUGHTER'S BED, SURROUNDED BY TOYS AND STUFFED CRITTERS.

Breaking out of the standard operating procedure you have created for yourself is a huge step toward a creative life. Cultivating a creative life means thinking and acting in new ways so you can be open to the possibilities around you.

YOU MUST DISRUPT YOUR NORMAL PATTERNS SO YOU CAN SEE THE WORLD WITH NEW EYES.

We often react to the world in predictable ways. Sometimes our behaviors become programmed, as if we are on autopilot. We put on our socks in the same order, follow the same routine in the shower, scoot around the house, and begin our day in a scripted pattern. These are the habits and patterns that we have created over many years.

My freshman year at art school, there was this teacher, you know, the teacher that has almost mythic status? His name was Al DeCredico (1944–2009). He was brilliant. His teaching techniques were designed to take the cocky, naïve nineteen-year-old freshman students and crack them wide open to the world and everything in it. How do you do that in a Drawing 101 class?

Here is how he did it: **he expected the unexpected**. He inspired his students to bypass the rational mind and the normal process of how we viewed drawing, creating, art, and life. His techniques were brutally simple—he taught us to seek surprises.

Near the beginning of the semester, he asked us to come back the following week with a self-portrait in charcoal on newsprint. We all dutifully created our masterpieces. Because of his legendary presence, everyone worked extra hard. When the next studio session rolled around, we nervously poured in, excited to show off our work. We pinned our work to the viewing wall.

Al walked in late to the drawing studio. The floors creaked. He scanned the wall. He pondered. He was quiet. He stood back, leaning on his cane. Then he did something that I will never forget. It was the harshest and most beautiful teaching technique I have ever seen. He walked right up to the wall and unpinned the first drawing on the far left. He flipped it over to inspect the back. He looked at it for what felt like twenty minutes but must have been twenty seconds; then he pinned it back on the wall, with the right side *facing the wall* so all we saw was the back of the paper. The

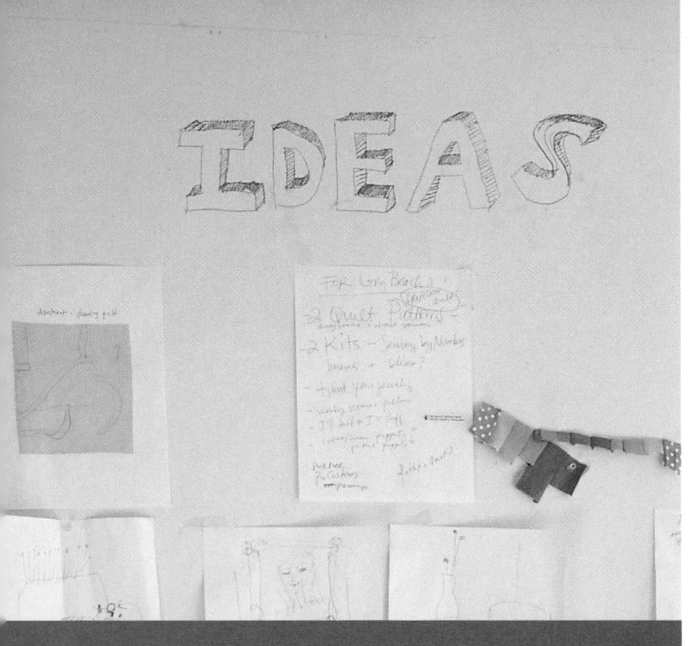

BE DISRUPTIVE OF YOUR CREATIVE PROCESS AND YOUR LIFE AND YOU WILL FIND A WELLSPRING OF RICHES AND FREEDOM. STEP OUTSIDE THE NORMAL. STEP OUTSIDE THE EXPECTED TO FIND YOUR CREATIVE SELF. BE CURIOUS.

drawing now revealed an empty off-white page with smudges and fingerprints. He slowly walked down the rest of the wall, turning each drawing over as he went. His big hands handled each piece respectfully and with care. At first glance, it seemed that hiding everyone's hard work was the most disrespectful thing he could possibly do. That wasn't his point.

He stood back, took a breath, and said, "Now. Let's begin." For the next few hours we discussed the merits and strengths of those strangely beautiful new drawings in front of us. We dove beneath expectation, convention, intention, and ego. We spoke about art as liberation from conscious thought. We discussed abstraction and pure form—pure mark making. The marks on the backs of the pages were incidental. They were accidents, mishaps, the leftovers of a process of drawing a self-portrait on the front, handling the paper, moving it with dirty fingers, erasing with a kneaded eraser.

Al taught us to seek the unexpected. He was disruptive. He helped people make unconventional choices and get beyond their ideas and limitations.

His homework was often like this: Turn on the shower, get in, and draw what you see. Draw with peanut butter. Draw with your eyes closed. Make a drawing without using anything found in the art supply store.

THIS WALL IS JUST OUTSIDE MY STUDIO. IT HAS BECOME AN ANNEXED IDEA AND INSPIRATION WALL. DRAW ON YOUR WALLS! PIN INTO YOUR WALLS. I WROTE IDEAS, BUT YOU COULD WRITE ANYTHING. CHOOSE AN AREA THAT CAN BE LESS PRECIOUS AND LET IT BE YOUR LAUNCHPAD.

So, today and while you are reading this book, do lots of unexpected things. Surprise yourself. Break your own rules. Leave the trail behind. Bypass your patterns and routines.

1. Do you always buy the same veggies at the grocery store? Go buy an eggplant or something in the store you have never even heard of or seen before.

2. Take a walk with your eyes closed. Just try it. Try to walk down your street, with a friend (to keep you safe), with your eyes closed.

3. For one day—all day—write and draw only with your nondominant hand.

4. Do you have an absolutely favorite quote? Grab a pencil and write it directly on your wall so you can see it every day. Draw on your walls. Break a simple rule.

WRITE YOUR FAVORITE QUOTE ON YOUR WALL IN PENCIL, SOMEWHERE YOU CAN SEE IT EVERY DAY. THIS IS WRITTEN ON MY STUDIO DOORWAY.

SPARK
11

Jar of Markers

THESE JARS HAVE BEEN ON OUR TABLE LIKE ARTFUL BOUQUETS FOR FIVE YEARS. THE PAPER IS ON A NEARBY BOOKSHELF. WE DRAW WITH THEM EVERY DAY.

No matter if your creative passion is playing guitar or glassblowing, you need a jar of markers or colored pencils on your dining table (or some other table that you sit at regularly). We have several at our house—one for markers, one for colored pencils, and one for plain yellow pencils and scissors. They have been there for five years. I use beautiful Japanese ceramic cups and mason jars to hold the markers. They sit in the center of the dining table where we eat every day, three times a day (plus snacks and homework), like an artful bouquet of creative possibility. Granted, I am a mom to small children, and granted, I have written that this is my very most favorite tip for fostering creativity in children. But doesn't it apply to grown-ups as well?

You know what these jars are? They are an invitation to creativity. Whenever we want to draw, sketch, or write, they are there. We don't have to go find the materials. The paper sits on a nearby shelf—within arm's reach of the table, we keep journals, drawing pads, and stacks of recycled printer paper.

No matter what your creative fantasy is, you need ready access to writing, doodling, planning, and sketching tools. Creativity can strike at any moment, and you want to be ready for it when it does. The jar of pencils is like a fishing line cast into a river—you're sitting by, waiting until you get a nibble. When you do, you'll be ready to catch it. One thing I have learned about my creative process is that if I don't jot down my ideas as they come to me, in that exact moment, I might lose them. Ideas are pretty ephemeral. They flit in; they float out. Sometimes … poof! They are gone.

> The jar of pencils is a butterfly net for those fleeting thoughts and ideas. If you can capture them in their pure, raw state, you have the makings of a new idea, a new beginning.

The jar of pens is an emblem, but it is also a reminder. The pens and pencils, always there, will quietly call to you, gently reminding you to listen to the call of your heart.

TEXTILE DESIGNER BARI ACKERMAN'S SCOTTSDALE, ARIZONA, STUDIO IS AS LOVELY AND FEMININE AS HER DESIGNS. EMBROIDERY FLOSS FILLS A CRYSTAL BOWL; BOLTS OF HER FABRIC BECKON FROM VINTAGE TRASH CANS (A GREAT STORAGE TIP). HER TOOLS ARE DISPLAYED IN A WAY THAT IS BOTH PRETTY AND EASILY ACCESSIBLE.

Do This

- We all need reminders. What are some other ways to remind yourself to listen to the little Spark today? Write yourself a Post-it note and put it on the bathroom mirror:

  I will take one risk.
  I will make a mess.
  I will make a cake.
  I will try something new.
  I will fail at something.

- Make a goal for yourself every week on a Post-it note, or write it directly on the wall. You can always paint over it.

- What other inspiring tools can be a metaphorical reminder for your creative life? What artful materials can you set in the middle of your table? Maybe you could place a jar of antique whisks on your kitchen counter? How about a bowl full of guitar picks on your coffee table? Think about having an emblem for your passion and create a little collection, shrine, or altar of objects to visually represent your Spark. Whatever inspires you, look at it every day. We all need reminders.

SPARK 12

Go Window Shopping

Retail, in our capitalist society, has cornered the market on creativity in so many ways. Big business means big money. Big retail brands have dollars and creative interns (armies of talented, unpaid college kids) and think tanks and more dollars and control groups and idea labs and more creative interns. Forget the actual goods—just think of merchandising, branding, and marketing. Stores are the new galleries. The creative aspect of consumerism is that we are all curating our own story through the things we buy. Whether we are conscious or unconscious of these choices, they tell a story about us to the world.

YOU ARE SURROUNDED BY A TAPESTRY OF RICHES EVERY DAY.

I, as a creative person, feel inspired just by getting dressed—just by which scarf I choose to wear with which pants. When I wander around my city and the world, I am looking at materials, relationships between things, objects, ideas. I am curious about the pageantry of this beautiful life—not just the beauty of the natural world (which inspires me daily), but also the pageantry of what we humans do here, the stuff that we make, sell, and buy. I have always been a huge fan of package design and international grocery stores. I love seeing the cultural differences in packaging and colors, the psychology of commerce.

ALEXANDRA MAW POURS LOVE AND VITALITY INTO EACH OF THE ORGANIC JUICES SHE CREATES FOR HER COMPANY, KALEIDOSCOPE JUICE, IN PHOENIX, ARIZONA. HER BUSINESS IS A VIBRANT, CREATIVE EXPRESSION SHE BUILT WITH HER MOTHER, ANDREA MAW.

I have as much deference for a beautifully designed plastic rice-paper pouch of Japanese udon noodles as I do an old teacup in a museum. They are both beautiful. They are both evidence of this life and how we humans navigate it.

You are surrounded by a tapestry of riches every day. See it. Be curious about the colors, the patterns, and the design of all of it. It will help you expand your thinking and engage with your senses in a different way.

Being creative means wandering through your life like an openhearted warrior, paying attention to the world around you. It means seeing with your senses, feeling your way through the world, and finding meaning in what you see. It means making your own meaning and looking at the world through squinted eyes, so lines become blurred and you see broad movements and contrasts more clearly.

You get to decide what is right for you. Not just in your creative pursuit, but also in the entire expression of your creative, beautiful self.

The world is your creation. The way you inhabit your life is a creative act.

Creativity isn't something you do; it is who you are.

It informs your decisions, your actions, your relationships, and your values.

Life is à la carte. There is no single right way. Rather, there are limitless, endless possibilities. It is as if you were standing in a gentle, clear stream. If you just open your hands as things float by, you can grab what you want. Leave the rest. Be in the stream of yourself and your life. Make decisions from your heart, from your highest self. Make decisions that are good for you, those you love, and the earth. Be open to possibility, opportunity, and the moment. Stand in the stream with your hands open to receive and you will be living a creative life.

- So today, go shopping! Go to the mall. Go to Anthropologie, Urban Outfitters, Nordstrom, Target, or Trader Joe's. Look around. Open your eyes to the giant creative engine that is using every resource it can to creatively sell you stuff. Go look at mannequins, displays, signage, advertising, and wall treatments. Look at the way merchandising tells a story that draws you in. Notice how the story of the brand is revealed through imagery, colors, textures, text, and graphics. Really look and be inspired. Notice what captivates your imagination. What inspires you? What jazzes you?
- Go to an international market: an Indian spice shop, a Japanese grocery store, or a Mexican market. Look at how different cultures approach package design. Look at how the natural world shows up in markets from different countries.

BEING A CREATIVE PERSON MEANS WAY MORE THAN MAKING COOL STUFF. IT IS A WAY OF BEING IN THE WORLD.

- Go to local places such as farmers' markets, small boutiques, and cafés. Investigate the vernacular style of your town. Find its voice. **This is an exercise in seeing creatively and seeing creativity.** If you can see it, you know it better and it can inform your spirit and your practice. Being a creative person means way more than making cool stuff. It is a way of being in the world.

SPARK

13

Get In Your Body

PHOENIX, ARIZONA, YOGA TEACHER ANTON MACKEY ENCOURAGES STUDENTS TO TURN OFF THEIR MINDS AND LOOK WITHIN BY CLOSING THEIR EYES AS THEY PRACTICE THEIR YOGA: "YOU DON'T NEED TO SEE THE POSE; YOU JUST NEED TO FEEL IT." TRUST YOUR BODY TO TAKE YOU WHERE YOU NEED TO GO.

Research shows that using your muscles also helps your mind. Studies reveal improved creative thinking after aerobic exercise. Regular exercise increases the number of tiny blood vessels that bring oxygen-rich blood to the brain and body.

In addition to the physical effects of exercise, sometimes you just need to get out of your head. The mind can be so noisy. That is one of the many reasons I love yoga. I go into the yoga studio, close my eyes, and let go. My teacher, Anton Mackey, turns up the music and I am free. I get out of my head. I am present in the moment. It is simple in that space—just me, my breath, and my moving body.

Some people get that feeling from running, hiking, cycling, or swimming. It is more than endorphins and blood flow—it is

space.

Space between yourself and your thoughts; space between each thought. Getting into your body through exercise creates stillness in your mind. Meditation is another way to find some quiet space. For creativity, it is important to turn off the incessant chatter of your mind and to bypass the intellect, to create a fresh place inside.

You might already be thinking that this is the coolest chapter in this book. Or you may be groaning, rolling your eyes, and thinking, "Harrumph … someone else making me feel bad that I don't exercise enough." That is not my intention. Today, you'll get into your body for the purposes of quieting your mind and tuning in to your heart for your creative life—not to lose weight, get healthy, or get in shape.

Our intelligence is a wonderful thing, but it can also make us rather stupid.

The mind often seeks the comfort of the rational solution, the safety of habits and the status quo. It's filled with those dudes that limit us: critic, judge, axman of dreams. Creativity comes from innocence, openness, curiosity, and playfulness. You can bypass your intellect (and all its limitations) by actually physically moving it aside with exercise.

The heart speaks in abundance, limitless possibility, dreams, and love. Pay attention to it. Get to know your heart. Start listening to it, so you get better at knowing what it's saying and what it wants.

SO MUCH OF A CREATIVE PRACTICE AND A CREATIVE LIFE IS BORN FROM BYPASSING THE MIND AND TUNING IN TO THE HEART.

Over time, you'll develop an on/off switch for your mind, so you can hear your heart, your soul, your spirit, God, your higher self, your little Spark, the universe, or any combination of words that resonates for you. Your rational mind doesn't always serve you. It can impede your intuition and the strong messages you are receiving. Learn to turn it off so you can get to the business of tending to your soul.

➤ Today, take a hike, a fast walk, a run, a yoga class, a spin class, or an aerobics class. Work hard. Breathe deeply. Lose your mind. The harder you work, the quieter your thoughts may become. You might find your thoughts going to the future or past. You may notice that you seek distractions from your physical discomfort. You may find only quiet and breath. Just be in the moment. I often have to write or take notes after I exercise because ideas come to me when I make space for myself and I quiet the constant stream of my usual thought process.

When your cheeks are rosy and you're covered in a light sweat, grab this book and a pen and see if anything new pops up.

➤ Here is what I found in my body today:

➤ Additionally, **go outside!**

Wander outside and take a walk. Breathe the air. Feel it in your body. Notice the smells of your street—the natural world—explore the textures, sounds, and smells. Let them fill your mind, heart, and senses. **Nature is spring cleaning for the soul!** It is one of my main sources of inspiration and grounding.

SPARK 14

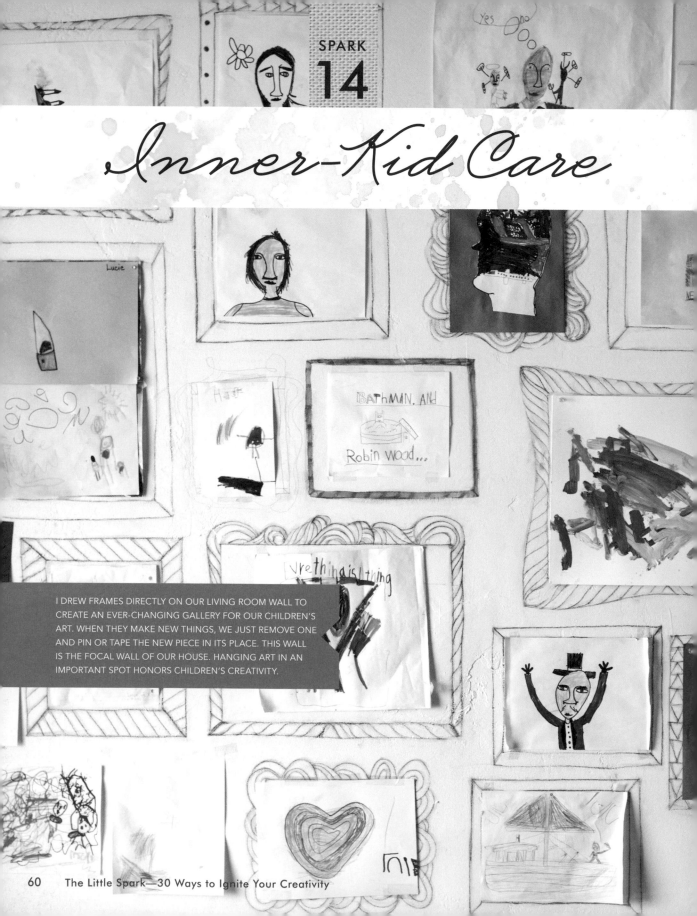

Inner-Kid Care

I DREW FRAMES DIRECTLY ON OUR LIVING ROOM WALL TO CREATE AN EVER-CHANGING GALLERY FOR OUR CHILDREN'S ART. WHEN THEY MAKE NEW THINGS, WE JUST REMOVE ONE AND PIN OR TAPE THE NEW PIECE IN ITS PLACE. THIS WALL IS THE FOCAL WALL OF OUR HOUSE. HANGING ART IN AN IMPORTANT SPOT HONORS CHILDREN'S CREATIVITY.

You need look no further than the bright, shining, creative kid you used to be to find the source of your creativity. She or he has been here all along. We have to talk about it at some point, and now is the time. How can I write a book with the sole purpose of enabling your creativity and helping you listen to your little Spark without figuring out when you lost it or covered it up? It has most likely just been hiding.

This is a simple exercise to uncover memories and release them. Give yourself about 20–30 minutes of quiet alone time in a comfortable spot. Read the following activity aloud. You can use your phone to record your reading, then play it back while you meditate.

Do This

Remembering the Spark

Sit quietly with your eyes closed. Breathe deeply—in through your nose, out through your nose. The breath brings you to the here and now and quiets the noisy mind.

Breathe for a few minutes until you feel connected to the ground beneath you, until your mind calms down. When you get there, ask yourself to remember images of your creative life as a child. What made you come alive? What was your favorite thing to do or make? What gave you that feeling of ecstatic joy, of focused and absorbed playtime? What did you love to do freely, with great joy and limitless energy? What do you see? How old were you? Were you alone or with someone? Where were you? Pay attention to the details. When you're ready, come back to your breath. Begin to feel your body in the room. Open your eyes. Write down your memories. You may have paragraphs to write or just a few snippets and glimpses.

See that kiddo with all that passion? All those ideas and dreams? That's you. See yourself as that child. Be as gentle with yourself as you would be with that young person.

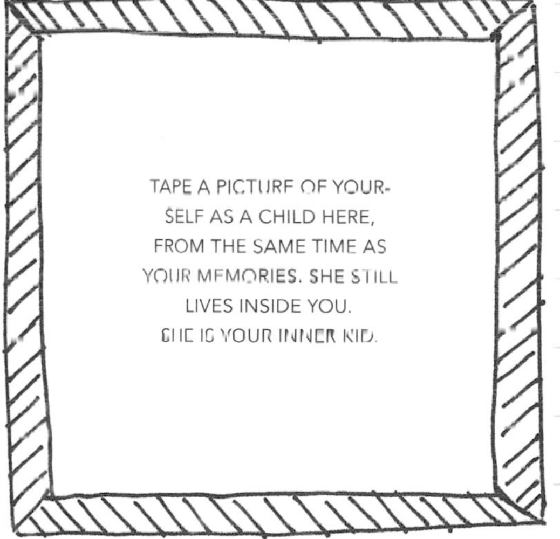

TAPE A PICTURE OF YOURSELF AS A CHILD HERE, FROM THE SAME TIME AS YOUR MEMORIES. SHE STILL LIVES INSIDE YOU. SHE IS YOUR INNER KID.

HERE IS WHAT MY SPARK LOOKED LIKE WHEN I WAS YOUNG:

Do This

What Happened to the Spark?

➤ Get comfortable again and breathe, as before. Ask yourself to remember what happened to that Spark. Where did it go? When did you stop listening? How old were you? What got in the way? Did someone or something take it away or dim its light? Did you become embarrassed of your joy, passion, or talent? Did someone tell you that you could never make any money and you should find a different path? Did people tell you that you weren't good at it? Did you believe them? Did you feel you weren't good enough? Be there. See the details. It may be uncomfortable, but stay with it. Then come back into the present moment, into your body. Open your eyes. Most likely, tears will coat your eyelashes as they coat mine as I write these words, because many of us carry so many feelings of inadequacy, fear, vulnerability, shame, or pain. Life has affected the little Spark for each and every one of us, even professional artists. Write down what you uncovered here:

HERE'S WHAT HAPPENED TO MY SPARK:

You are probably feeling something now. It may feel tender or fragile, painful or joyful. Write it down. Begin to release the story that was written over your Spark, the story that was inscribed into your heart. Let it go. Cry if you need to.

Some of that yucky stuff you may have just unearthed is called shame. Shame comes from feeling fundamentally inadequate, from feeling flawed or not good enough. I *strongly* urge you to find and watch Brené Brown's TED Talks (available on YouTube) on vulnerability and shame. (Watch the vulnerability talk first.) Maybe do that today. I have watched her talks twenty times. She has changed my life. I recommend that you get her books, too.

If you bring your shame into the light, it can't lurk and haunt you from within. Shame is a powerful emotion. It seeks to remain hidden. It protects itself so you can't find it. But the moment you become aware of it nestling in the softest and most private inner folds of your heart is the moment you begin to lessen its power over you. It begins to crawl away. It skulks off.

Write down all of it. Bringing it into the light will help you move on and dive more deeply into your creative practice. That feeling might always be there to some extent, but once you name it and call it out, you have power over it, instead of the other way around.

- What negative messages have you developed about yourself over the years? Maybe you have said these things to yourself or learned them from others. For example, "I am clumsy," or "I can't make any money being creative," or "I can't even draw a stick figure!" Write them down here:

NEGATIVE SELF-TALK:

NOW, GRAB A HUGE, FAT SHARPIE MARKER AND CROSS THOSE OUT!

- Replace those negative messages with some others. Take each of the negative messages and write the opposite. If you wrote, "I am clumsy," change it to "I am graceful." "I can't make any money being creative" becomes "I have a thriving business based on my creativity." Do that here:

POSITIVE SELF TALK:

Take some time to process what you have learned about yourself. Keep this book or a journal with you because you may have more thoughts you want to write down. Good work.

SPARK 15

Doubt

GIN BLOSSOMS GUITARIST SCOTTY JOHNSON OFTEN SITS AT HIS PIANO WHEN HE WANTS TO WARM UP AND GET INTO THE FLOW. BECAUSE THE PIANO IS HIS SECOND INSTRUMENT AND NOT HIS FIRST LOVE, HE FEELS FREE TO PLAY AROUND AND EXPLORE.

ANONYMOUS

Many of us hold on to doubt so we don't allow ourselves to build a ladder with duct tape and backyard twigs to get us to the moon. But you can, you know. You can build that ladder with your own two hands, sheer excitement, and intention if you trust the process and take the first step.

One of the most important ways we can overcome self-doubt is to make peace with it. **Befriend your doubt.** Notice when it shows up. Gently honor it like an old friend. Maybe even nicely ask your doubt to leave. When we are busy trying to get rid of something, we expend a lot of energy and we are unwittingly feeding it.

FOUR WAYS TO REMOVE DOUBT

Rituals

We don't have enough rituals in our modern culture, but our ancestors did. Use ritual to honor the transition into your creative activity. A ritual can be a simple thing we use as a tool to step into a more personal, internal space. It may be dark chocolate. It may be a moment of gratitude for the blessings of today. It may be a simple prayer in which you ask for strength and courage and that you work to your highest and best good. Maybe you say, "Today I will make a mess, play, and have fun." I burn sage (smudge) before I work (a Native American ritual), to clear the energy and start fresh.

Music

Music takes me into myself and out of my head. I'll tell you a little nerdy secret: since I was about 14 years old, anytime I have started painting or working in my studio, I have put on pianist George Winston's *December* album. Every time. It is the thread that runs through my creative life. It grounds and centers me. Because I have been using it as a tool to enter my creative space for 27 years, it keeps me in touch with the girl who dreamed really big in her studio, making big abstract paintings on the studio floor into the wee hours of the morning. It reminds me that the reason I make things is because of that girl—that girl in me who believes in herself so much. The girl who made ten-foot abstract paintings on the floor with her bare hands and acrylic paint. The naïve girl filled with love, longing, and expression. The girl who didn't think "no" was an option. The girl who felt the tender beauty and transience of this life and wanted to paint that feeling. I am still that girl. I stand in her shoes. She is my bedrock. I get to her with the help of George Winston's somber, lyrical piano music. And when I am in the flow, I turn off George and get my groovin' playlist out and dance and sing like a kid.

Affirmations

Affirmations are a great way to stay present and grounded (and away from self-doubt).

I am beautiful. I am talented. I am smart. I am creative. I am kind. I am generous. I can do anything. And my favorite: **I am enough**. Get into the habit of saying affirmations to yourself daily or as needed. Be sure to choose affirmations that you actually believe about yourself.

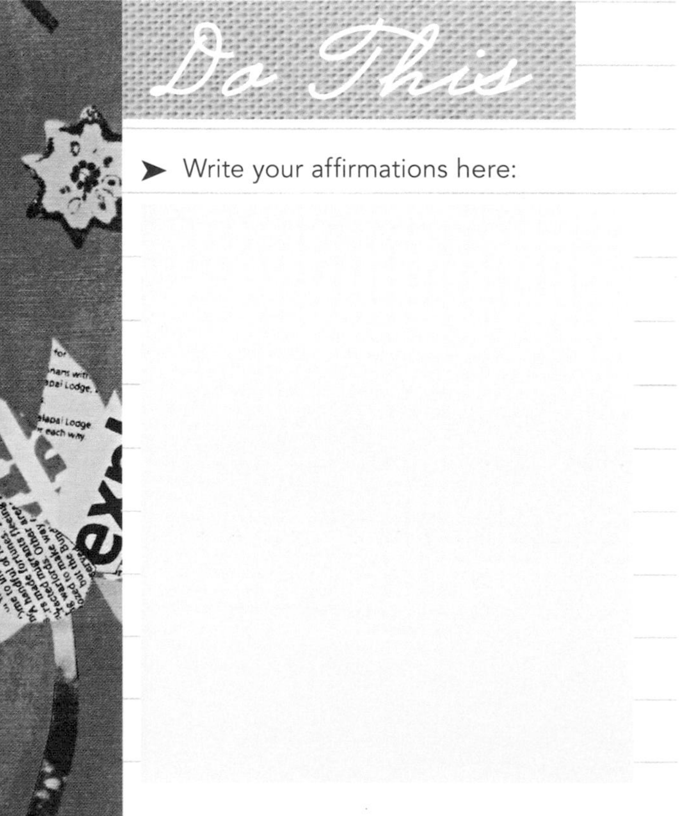

Do This
➤ Write your affirmations here:

Talismans

A talisman is an object believed to contain certain magical properties that may provide good luck or fortune. Most pottery folks have Kiln Gods. You might spy a weird creature or figure made from clay scraps sitting on top of their kiln. It has nothing to do with religion, but rather is meant as a superstitious protection of each firing of the kiln so nothing cracks or explodes. In Japanese restaurants you'll see that cat with his paw in the air, *maneki-neko*—the Beckoning Cat. It is a good-luck charm. The Chinese have used carved sculptures of Foo Dogs as protection for front doors for millennia.

Talismans provide as much help to us as we believe they do—all in the name of good fortune and protection. As I type, I'm wearing the *writing mala* (bracelet) I designed (and my friend Logan Milliken, owner of Silver & Sage Jewelry, made for me) with feldspar, rose quartz, and jasper. I chose these stones to promote truth, clarity, and love. It's like I'm wearing a superpower; I feel like Wonder Woman as I write. Do you have a feel-good object? A special object or piece of jewelry that can be used to boost confidence, clarity, love—anything? It will help you get in the flow, like an external boost of confidence and intention.

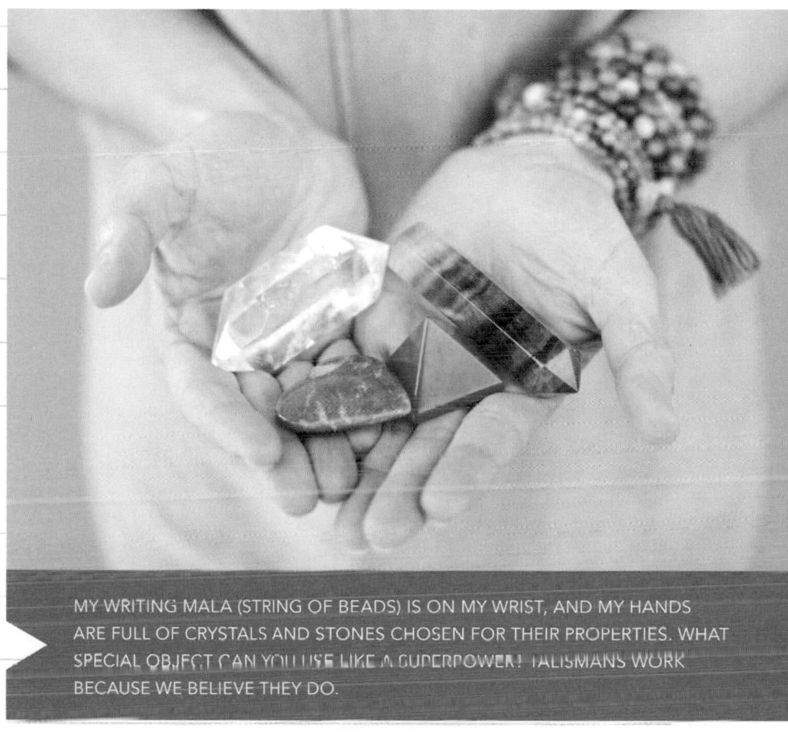

MY WRITING MALA (STRING OF BEADS) IS ON MY WRIST, AND MY HANDS ARE FULL OF CRYSTALS AND STONES CHOSEN FOR THEIR PROPERTIES. WHAT SPECIAL OBJECT CAN YOU USE LIKE A SUPERPOWER? TALISMANS WORK BECAUSE WE BELIEVE THEY DO.

Do This

- Think about creating a ritual or talisman for your creative practice. Write about it here:

- Make a playlist of your favorite music. What music gets you in the mood to be creative?

SPARK 16

Have a Secret

MY ALL-TIME FAVORITE ARTIST IS MY DEAR OLD FRIEND, BIRMINGHAM, ALABAMA, ARTIST DOUG BAULOS. HIS IS AN ART OF SECRET KEEPING, MYSTERY, AND HUMANNESS. HE FINDS HIS WORK IN LAYERS. HE IS A POET—A SOUL MECHANIC. HE DOESN'T REVEAL ALL OF HIS HAND—EVER. YET HE REVEALS A LOT BY WHAT HE KEEPS UNKNOWN, BY WHAT HE DOESN'T SAY.

Photo by Doug Baulos

I was an eighteen-year-old freshman at the Rhode Island School of Design when I received the following homework assignment. My Two-Dimensional Design teacher, Jack Massey, asked us to do something very simple: have a secret.

This is what he told us to do:

Do something alone, just for you, by yourself, in the middle of nowhere, in a hidden place or out in the world—with no one else around. You can make a piece of art, do a performance or action, dance, write something, or make a site-specific installation. Whatever it is, it is your secret. Don't tell anyone about it or talk about it—to anyone—ever.

That was ages before social media, before we advertised our every thought on Facebook, before we became increasingly entwined with externalizing our lives.

I don't remember what I did for Jack's assignment. I feel like it involved a bridge near the water on Wickenden Street. Certainly, we didn't show up with anything in class to discuss or critique the next week, because we were all just holding on to our secrets. If you were a student interested in *not* doing homework, then this was the assignment of your dreams. You could do nothing and no one would ever know.

Jack was teaching us to work just for ourselves and not for some external reward. He gave us this very important lesson:

THE REWARD IS INSIDE US.

Creativity generally yields something that we share with others—a piece of music, a piece of jewelry, a painting, or a photo. Creative people tend to want to share their work and yet tend to be shy about that sharing. Your own creative voice can get a bit clouded by all the other voices you hear from peers and teachers. It can become confusing and difficult to listen to your own voice.

For me, Jack's assignment was a lesson in holding something sacred. Often when you talk about things and ideas, it fuels and connects you. But sometimes it diminishes the power of something special that you are hatching inside your heart or mind. Sometimes you need to sit with your secret treasure and let its embers warm you from the inside and just feel the glow.

We are all creating our own reality every day. We speak and communicate to share the contents of our lives, but it is all very personal. There are times when we just need to be pregnant. If you are a woman and have been pregnant you know exactly what I am describing here. There may be a day, an hour, a week, a month, or even longer that you are pregnant, and it is all yours. You are carrying a new life inside your body, and yet no one knows. You haven't told anyone for a variety of reasons. And it feels so private. My friend Kerry loved that time. She savored those sacred days before she shared her pregnancy and it became a public event instead of just hers.

There are times when you need to be similarly pregnant with your own creativity and just sit with that private experience. Just be with the tiny Spark. Sit still and don't shout it out—just be. There is so much power in not talking about things. They become more real in your mind, more concrete, more personal.

Photo by Doug Baulos

Do This

- The Have a Secret lesson is a powerful one. Do it today. See what you find. Honor your creative moment, whatever it looks like. And then just percolate. Feel it. Don't tweet it, Instagram it, Facebook it, or blog about it. Don't tell your spouse or best friend. Don't tell your parents or children.

JUST BE ALONE WITH IT.

Inspiration

IN MY STUDIO, I PUT MY FAVORITE STUFF OUT SO I CAN SEE IT AND IT CAN INVITE ME. I LOVE THE COLOR OF DENIM AND MY STACK OF SOMBER JAPANESE TEXTILES THAT I HOARD. I KEEP SKEINS OF RECYCLED SILK SARI RIBBON FROM LEILANI ARTS OUT SO I CAN BE INSPIRED BY THE RICH COLORS.

Photo by Logan Milliken

LOGAN MILLIKEN, OF SILVER & SAGE JEWELRY, IS INSPIRED BY THE CONNECTION SHE MAKES NOT JUST WITH HER BEADS BUT WITH THE ARTISANS SHE SUPPORTS AROUND THE WORLD.

Photo by Allison V. Smith

ADAM RAYMONT IS A PAINTER BASED IN BERLIN AND NEW YORK. "MOVING THINGS AROUND MAKES THINGS FRESH AND CREATES NEW RELATIONSHIPS WHICH MIGHT KICK OFF A NEW IDEA," HE EXPLAINS. HERE IS HIS STUDIO—LAYERED WITH WORKS IN PROGRESS.

FOLLOW FIREFLIES

Inspiration is everywhere you look. It can be commonplace or holy. It can catch you unaware and take away your breath. It can leave you speechless. How often have you been playing around online, and twenty minutes later you snap back into reality after you were utterly absorbed by an interesting article or video?

In our modern world, we are bombarded daily with many varieties of images. How you look at them helps you find the keepers, the good stuff you need to light your way. These are the fireflies. If you see them, it is up to you to stop what you're doing and wander into the yard.

When we step into a life of chasing the fireflies of inspiration, we are more able to get into a creative space. By doing this, we create a fluency between our so-called normal life and our creative life. Pretty soon, they begin to merge. Our life begins to shimmer, glow, sparkle, and radiate with creative energy.

> Inspiration is fuel for the little Spark. It is the lamplighter, the flame maker, the firefly. It is the lighthouse. We cultivate it simply by being open to it.

If you walk around the world with an open heart (not guarded or protected), then you will be more available to inspiration. Inspiration is often just a pebble thrown onto the path. It is up to you to stop, stoop down, and investigate it.

BE CURIOUS IN YOUR LIFE.

CYNDI COON'S WHOLE HOUSE IS FILLED WITH LITTLE MOMENTS OF INSPIRATION.

SLOW DOWN

Stop rushing hither and yon. Slow down. Be mindful. If you are racing through life to get from one item on your to-do list to the next, then you are missing half the beauty right in front of you. A mindfulness practice develops slowly, but it starts by just paying attention to whatever it is you are doing, whenever you are doing it. If you are making dinner, make dinner. If you are doing homework with your kids, do homework. If you are cleaning, clean. We are so often pulled to our future or past thoughts that we can miss the simplicity of this exquisite moment. Inspiration is easily overlooked if you are engaged in mental note taking and to-do lists.

UNPLUG

Sometimes, inspiration comes from a blog or a Pinterest board or something you found via social media. But often, the cacophony of tweets and chirps and bits and bytes that bombard you every day also takes you out of the moment. Sometimes you stare at the screen too long and your eyes can barely readjust to this world. Social media dislocate us even as they connect us. Try to unplug from all social media—even if it is just for short periods of time. Then you can be more connected to the real world and the moments that are right in front of you.

DAYDREAM

Daydreaming is an active creative process. It can yield some wonderful fruits. Let your mind wander when it needs to. Mine wanders like crazy when I tuck my kids into bed. Some of my greatest inspiration happens in my son's bed, staring at the lit-up fish tank in the dark, quiet room. I get hooked into an idea or a thought and I follow it. Often I will stumble out of their bedrooms and run to the computer to write.

The creative solution takes patience. You have to wait for it. Commonly it comes when you look the other way instead of looking for it. Inspiration often involves a multisensory experience and quiet or solitude.

HAVE A NET

No matter how you get to your inspiration, the main recommendation I have for you is this: have a net.

Inspiration is ephemeral and fleeting—it comes and goes within seconds. Do yourself a favor and always have a net to catch it. For me, that might be dictating notes to Siri on my iPhone in a parking lot. It might mean having a pen and paper next to your bed, kitchen sink, shower—wherever you commonly daydream. This idea is discussed in more depth in Spark 11: Jar of Markers (page 48).

Do This

➤ What inspires you? What are you curious about?

➤ How can you get more inspiration? Where do you usually find your inspiration?

➤ Who are your creative superheroes? They may be friends, teachers, strangers, or leading artists or craftspeople in your field. Who inspires you?

As time passes, you may need the gentle reminders of your passion and inspiration. Sometimes, the further you get into something, the more help you need. When the excitement wears off, you might need to dip into your bag of tricks to find the fireflies. It's okay to get bored along your path, or feel uninspired, or too tired some days. It's okay if you don't feel nonstop inspiration and desire for your creative life every day. That's normal. Just keep going, by using your toolbox and the steps outlined in this book—take the day off, go see a movie, go hang out with friends, think about who and what inspires you, and get connected again.

SPARK

18

The Pleasure Principle

I LEARNED TO KNIT IN FOURTH GRADE FROM MY GRANDMOTHER'S NEIGHBOR, MARION EPSTEIN (MANNY) AND FROM MRS. BROUGHTON, WHO WOULD TEACH US AFTER SCHOOL. EVER SINCE, KNITTING HAS SOOTHED MY SOUL. EVEN IN ART SCHOOL, I WOULD COME HOME FROM THE INTELLECTUAL RIGORS OF THE STUDIO AND CLIMB IN MY BED WITH SKEINS OF COLORFUL CHENILLE. I'D KNIT SCARVES AND READ ***MARTHA STEWART LIVING*** MAGAZINE LIKE IT WAS SOME FORBIDDEN PLEASURE. CRAFTING SEEMED LIKE A DIRTY SECRET TO ME THEN, BUT IT KEPT ME SANE IN THE IVORY TOWER.

Photo by Amber Corcoran

"Let the beauty of what you love be what you do."

RUMI

What makes you feel good? Why would you need to be reminded about seeking pleasure? We are all so good at that, right? No, not really. But you once were. And certainly you knew what made you happy as a child.

When was the last time you watched a seven-year-old, or a four-year-old, at play? I do every day. Here is what it looks like: they flit, they fly, they wander passionately from one creative enterprise to the next. Now playing with tiny plastic Littlest Pet Shop critters, now drawing, now LEGO, now back to Pet Shops, and on it goes. Constant desire. Constant movement. Constant momentum, even when they take breaks: Look! Here's a roll of duct tape! Look! I can write my own comic book! Look! Ice cream! Pleasure, pleasure, pleasure the whole way through. Children seek pleasure at every turn. They don't need reminders about how to play, how to have fun, or how to make room for themselves. They know what feels good.

And so should you. Your life is full and, no doubt, you have your hands full—with work, family, and other responsibilities. You probably don't take many moments to check in with your desires because you are so busy worrying about everyone else's. You may think that if you run around and take care of everyone else you are doing good and being good and all is right with the world. In some senses, that is true. But in other ways, it isn't.

What about yourself? About five years ago, after a few sessions, my new therapist asked me to make a list of my needs and wants. I looked at her blankly. I was confused. I went home and came back the next week and she had to explain it to me again. That time, I wrote a list and it looked like this:

I want my husband to __________. I need more time to __________ and if he would just __________ I could do that.

I didn't understand my needs and wants—I was codependent and enmeshed with my husband. I couldn't see myself or my desires because I was so preoccupied with whatever I thought he wasn't doing. It was all my stuff, but I made it about him so I didn't have to see myself at all, so I didn't have to deal with the heaps of unresolved feelings and urges inside me.

Competing for resources (time or money) is a common problem—it's easy to feel that there simply isn't enough time in the day to do everything we want to do. Some people may compete for resources with their partner: *if you go on that four-hour bike ride, then I'm going to go hike!* And on and on it goes. Regardless of whether or not you have a partner, children, a job, or an ailing parent, you have to decide how to allot your limited resources.

Responsibilities, financial pressures, plans—these are the reasons we forget to play and have fun. All of this can shred the fabric of the creative self because it is really important and it takes time and energy.

UNLESS

YOU → begin to uncover yourself from the bottom of the heaping, mountainous pile of your obligations and busyness, you might not get a crack of time to cultivate your creative self.

That is why you need to get in touch again with what feels good, just for you. If you can begin to discover and uncover *your* desire, you can pursue the Spark.

Do This

➤ So, what feels good? What do you want? How can you play? Explore your desires below. Begin to excavate the stuff that is just yours—not for anyone else or because of anyone else. In the space below, write your wants, not your have-tos, and not your wants for someone else (your spouse, your family), just your wants for *you*. (In the next chapter you will use this list to make something really cool.)

WHAT FEELS GOOD?

WHAT DO YOU WANT?

HOW CAN YOU PLAY?

SPARK

19

Make a Vision Board

Believe.

YOU'RE HIRED!

I'm living on less.
But I'm living more.

Inspired Reading

IN THE MIDDLE OF MY VISION BOARD FROM FOUR YEARS AGO IS A WOMAN I IMAGINED TO BE A TEXTILE DESIGNER IN INDIA. I HAD NO IDEA I WOULD EVEN START MY COMPANY, SUCH DESIGNS, WHEN I MADE THIS BOARD AND NO CLUE I WOULD BECOME A FABRIC DESIGNER! BUT MY UNCONSCIOUS MIND DID.

Awakening Mosaic Maven

OPEN YOUR EYES TO A NEW YOU

WHAT DO YOU WANT

LEARN

My creativity has no boundaries. It's ALWAYS ON.

Give & Save More!

SAVE

A vision board is simply a collage of images you pull from magazines and other places and paste to a board. This exercise puts you directly in touch with your desires. It leaves you with a visual inventory of all the stuff that bubbles up from your unconscious mind and heart to illuminate your path and remind you of what you want. I make vision boards at least twice a year and have for almost a decade. The boards can be as artistic or simple as you want. Mine tend to be bare bones.

The amazing thing about vision boards is that I have never made one that didn't come true. What you put on your board will show up in your life. It will be created in your life through your intention.

YOU WILL MANIFEST WHAT IS ON YOUR BOARD.

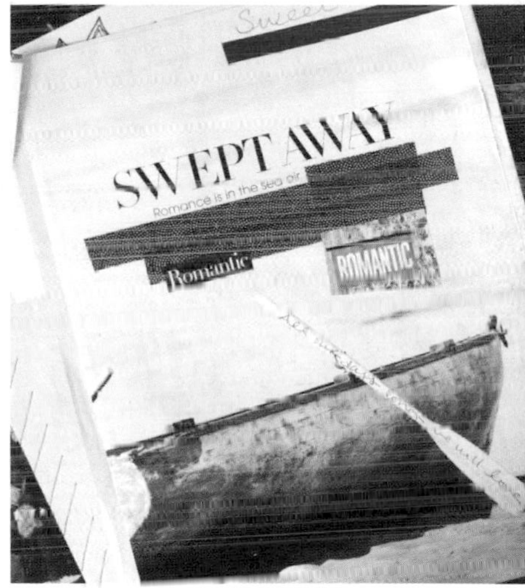

A PAGE FROM ONE OF CYNDI COON'S ARTFUL, INSPIRING VISION JOURNALS

You create a doorway to achieving your desires and your potential by giving your intention a voice. Your intention becomes a prayer.

> To make a vision board, tune in to your heart and soul. Sidestep your mind by banishing your inner critic, judge, and editor. Those parts of yourself are not welcome for this exercise. Ask them to leave the building. Why? Because you are only going to be listening to your desire. Not your desire for your partner, your children, your friends, or your family. Just your desire, for you.

HERE IS MY BEAUTIFUL INTERIOR DESIGNER MOM, RHONDA GREENBERG, WITH HER ARTFUL BUTTERFLY VISION BOARD.

Do This

Make a Vision Board

MATERIALS

- Scissors
- Gluestick
- Foamcore board (or any other board) in any size you like (20″ × 30″ is a good size)
- 6–10 magazines about varying topics that interest you (*O, The Oprah Magazine,* rocks for vision boards!)
- Family photos or any scraps of materials that you want to add

As you are looking at magazines, don't "should" on yourself—no "I *should* pick this image" or "I *should* want that one."

No critiquing your choices or urges. When you see something you like, rip it out. It is simple. **If you have no idea why you are ripping an image, rip it anyway.** Sometimes we aren't always aware of our own greatness or even what awaits us. Using pleasure and desire as a guide keeps you in your heart and soul and out of your editor and judge. Many times I will have an urge to rip a picture of, say, a Caribbean beach, and my inner editor will jump in and say, "What? You can't afford to take your family there!" I have learned to notice that voice and tune it out.

So, for an hour, rip or cut out images. Then for the next hour, paste them down.

You aren't making art. Remove your notions of how pretty your board will look, how perfect, and let it just be however it is. That being said, each board will be beautiful and full of meaning because it comes from you. My mom makes the most artful boards—one was shaped like a butterfly and filled with color and family. My friend, artist Cyndi Coon, makes vision journals. Each page represents a different topic she is working on. You might explore that later, as well.

Put your board in a spot where you can see it every day. After you look at your board and assimilate its wisdom, you may notice some themes. In a week, a month, or a year you will look at your board and realize that whether you knew what it meant at the time of its creation or not, you have accomplished most if not all of what is on your board. Each of my children showed up on my board before I was even pregnant with them and without me knowing I was ready. Such is the power of a vision board and honoring the wisdom that comes from deep within.

Repeat this exercise anytime you feel that you need a boost of direction or inspiration. I lead vision board groups. It is a great activity to share with friends. Ask everyone to bring drinks and snacks to share. Get some boards and gluesticks. Each person will bring magazines. It is interesting how even though we are chatting with friends as we share this activity, our boards end up filled with meaning. In some ways, the conversation and friendly chatter help us move out of our inner editor. New Year's is a great time to make a new board for setting your intentions for the new year. In my family, we make a family board on New Year's Day as well.

SPARK

20

Create a Mission Statement

ALEXANDRA MAW HOLDING HEAPS OF WHEATGRASS IN HER JUICE BAR, KALEIDOSCOPE JUICE, IN PHOENIX, ARIZONA

"The grass is greenest
where you water it."

NEIL BARRINGHAM

You know those people who seem to be floating on air, gliding along, joyful, content, connected? And you know how you think, "Hmmm, I'd like to be her. She seems to have it going on!" Well, guess what? Her life isn't better than yours or probably much different, but she's watering her grass. She feeds her Spark. You can see it in people when they are living a passionate life, and it makes you want it, too.

Your mission statement is one way to water your grass. Your intentions, thoughts, and desires will carry you along. Your grass might start small—just a galvanized tin bucket of happy wheatgrass sitting on your kitchen counter—but you'll have a healthy lawn in no time.

In this chapter we'll write a so-called non-business "business" plan—a creative mission statement. But first, let's smash your fantasy.

So, exactly what do you think a "creative life" looks like? Close your eyes. Take a deep breath. Picture it in your mind. Okay, got it? Great. Now toss that image out the window. Next, what does your creative process look like in your fantasy? Now chuck that one out the window, too—especially that one. Let it go!

Confused yet? Well, you'll need your dreams, your desires, and your intuitions to guide you on your path to a more creative life. What you won't need are your projections and fantasies of Photoshopped perfectionism, all tied up in a pretty bow and stylized like a cool magazine lifestyle shot. Smash those ideas to bits. Let them go. They will just get in your way. You want your life to be richer than a credit card ad, don't you? You want your dream to have more depth and texture than your friend's latest post on Facebook. How could you ever live up to fake, overblown, perfect fantasies? Would you even want to? I'm all for reaching for the moon, and healthy examples of working, productive, creative role models can help us realize that our dreams are attainable. But you have to start with your feet on the earth, even as you reach for the stars.

YOUR MISSION STATEMENT IS ONE WAY TO WATER YOUR GRASS.

Maybe you can't yet envision a creative life. You may not even know what a creative life looks like. That's okay. You can start right here. Look back into your family history. Is there a passionate person there? Someone who inspired you? Did your grandma love to can peaches in the heat of her summer kitchen? Did you have an uncle who tinkered away in the garage making wooden benches?

WHAT CAN YOU RECALL AS YOUR FIRST INSPIRATION?

Do you have an aunt who's a painter? An actor? A dancer? What can you recall as your first inspiration? A trip to the museum? The ballet? A particular chef? Picture people you know who have found purpose, pleasure, passion, and quietude in their creativity. Picture in your mind your friends who water their grass. Close your eyes and picture yourself in your creative life. See as many details as you can. Be specific.

JAMES BEARD AWARD–WINNING CHEF CHRIS BIANCO IN HIS NEWEST PIZZERIA BIANCO IN PHOENIX, ARIZONA. HIS MOTHER, FRANCESCA, PAINTED THESE LOVELY WATERCOLOR RECIPES. HIS FATHER IS ALSO A PAINTER. CHRIS'S SPARK BEGAN WITH THEM.

Start right here, right now, from your heart. Take a deep breath. Sit still in a quiet room. Focus on what you really want. This exercise can be done a few times until you feel like you are getting close to what you really want but still perhaps feel weird about verbalizing.

➤ Use one word to describe what *your* unique creative path looks like:

➤ One word to describe how it feels, or how you imagine it feels, to be on that creative path.

➤ How about two words?

➤ Write it as a sentence:

➤ Write a mission statement. Set your intentions right here on this page. Write it in the present tense and in first person. Be as specific as you can. Include details.

Example: *I am learning modern dance at a local dance studio. I feel competent and alive. I perform with the group on stage. I feel graceful in my skin. I feel content and peaceful. My whole life is transforming as I open up to my passion.*

➤ Use nice penmanship and write your statement on a pretty piece of paper. Or type it out on the computer in a cool font. Put your mission statement where you can see it every day. It will be there to guide you.

SPARK 21

Fear

Fear has been my companion since I was young. It is part of the reason I am an artist. Creativity is my own version of antianxiety meds. It's a self-made panacea and it's usually effective. The creative act is a resounding yes to life and everything in it. With each yes you beat back the fear—yes to this moment and to beauty, yes to witnessing and recording this life, yes to strength, ability, and willpower. You can't stay stuck in your fear if you are already wandering to your next creative project. Creativity is hope. There are really only two emotions—love and fear. We slip between the two.

FEAR IS THE BOILER ROOM IN THE BASEMENT OF YOUR CREATIVITY.

Fears will come. They always do. They are, in part, the furnace for your creative urges. Fear is the boiler room in the basement of your creativity. The same logs of imagination that fuel the fire of your fears also fuel your creativity. Those wildly scary stories you tell yourself that give you anxiety attacks come from the same source (your imagination) that helps you create wildly imaginative works of art.

"I live a creative life, and you can't be creative without being vulnerable. I believe that Creativity and Fear are basically conjoined twins; they share all the same major organs, and cannot be separated, one from the other, without killing them both. And you don't want to murder Creativity just to destroy Fear!"

ELIZABETH GILBERT

DISAPPEARING BEES

Life in our modern world is fraught with anxieties. Our fears are real. Our time here on earth is finite. Stuff happens. We are watching the glaciers melt and the pollinator bees disappear. Instead of feeding your fear and becoming immobilized by it, you can get to work. The creative act is the opposite of fear, because to create means to believe in the here and now. Being creative is an answer for right now. This moment, as the pollinator bees are dying, you are still here. So, what will you make today? Make something big or small. Be a rock thrown into the pond of existence. Be the answer to your fear. Choose love.

> Dream big. If your dreams don't scare you, they aren't big enough.

Creativity takes courage. It takes courage to be who you are. It takes courage to step into the unknown, to dig around in your soul and see what you find, to follow your passion, to start something new.

TWO WAYS TO BE BRAVE

Remain a Beginner

It may help you be brave if you remember that you're only expected to be a beginner. Pursue what Zen masters call "beginner's mind," or *shoshin*, a Zen Buddhist concept referring to a certain playful openness and lack of preconceptions as you work. As noted Zen teacher Shunryu Suzuki explains, "In the beginner's mind there are many possibilities; in the expert's mind there are few." When the pressure of performing is off, you can laugh at yourself and act silly—you are free to explore and play.

Fake It 'til You Make It

In her June 2012 TED Talk, Amy Cuddy spoke about her research into body language. (Watch it on YouTube.) She offered what she called a "free, no-tech life hack" called "power posing."

She spoke about the impact our body posture has on our success. For her experiment, one group of subjects sat with their shoulders slouched forward and heads down, making themselves small. Another group was instructed to take "power poses" and increase their body size by spreading their arms, chest, and legs wide to occupy space. Both groups stayed in their poses for two minutes before a job interview.

Her findings were amazing. Both groups had notable hormonal changes. The slouchers didn't get the jobs they applied for. The power posers did. Cuddy's research shows us is that we can actually rewire our minds, simply by changing our posture.

> Instead of feeling confident inside first, sometimes we can fake it on the outside and we will feel the effects.

This will help us be more productive and confident as we pursue our creativity.

Cuddy tells people: in a private place, stand tall in a pose with your hands on your hips for two minutes. Power pose before a meeting or class or whenever you need a confidence boost. The goal is to cause your hormones to kick up before your meeting so you feel empowered—even if it's fake. As Cuddy said, "Fake it 'til you become it." Practice your power pose and see how it makes you feel.

Do This

What are you afraid of about your creative path? Seriously afraid of?

- Write it down on a slip of paper. Take a deep breath and exhale it. Take that slip of paper to the shredder or the fireplace and let it go.
- Ask yourself: *What's the payoff for hanging on to my fears?*

I STARTED TAKING MODERN DANCE AT AGE 41. THE OTHER WOMEN IN THE CLASS ARE ALL MUCH OLDER THAN I AM. WE ARE SO BRAVE. FEW OF US HAVE A BACKGROUND IN DANCE, BUT WE SHOW UP EACH WEEK LISTENING TO THE SPARK, FULL OF GRACE AND DESIRE. "POWER POSING" LOOKS A LOT LIKE WHAT WE ARE DOING HERE: HANDS UP HIGH, TAKING UP A LOT OF SPACE.

SPARK 22

Find Your Voice

I CULTIVATED THIS FABRIC DESIGN FROM MY LIFE AS A PAINTER. THE PAINTBRUSHES BECAME THE ARTISTIC STORYLINE OF MY FABRIC LINE **PAINT!** FOR WINDHAM FABRICS. USE FAMILIAR ICONS TO TELL YOUR STORY.

> "You have to leave the city of your comfort and go into the wilderness of your intuition. What you'll discover will be wonderful. What you'll discover is yourself."
>
> ALAN ALDA

Living as a creative person calls on you to be exactly who you are. No matter what you do in your creative life, you will bring all of you to it. Creativity needs a subject. The subject of your creative life is you. You bring your senses, awareness, experience, and story with you.

As you figure out your preferences and desires, you will be cultivating what is called your creative *voice*. Your voice is a combination of your style, experience, work, and subject matter.

People will feel your joy, love, and excitement in your creations. They will also feel your pain, confusion, struggle, and fear. The things you make speak for you in the world. Why bother making a painting or a song if you could just say it with words? Art picks up where words stop. Creative expression is there to communicate the stuff in your heart that is so tender that you don't have a voice for it. The creative product, whether a poem or clay bowl, is infused with your spirit. Everything you create is a self-portrait. The richness you mine for your subject is your own psyche. As Bono of U2 so beautifully put it, "the great songs kind of write you," not the other way around. Let your work move through you; let it use you to speak. Staying open to it will allow you to become kind of like a pitcher. The water will pour from you.

EVERYTHING YOU CREATE IS A SELF-PORTRAIT

If you're lucky, you can shed the crap that spews from the ego—the stuff that keeps you safe, stuck, or living someone else's dream of your life. That stuff keeps you from yourself. Being comfortable in your own skin helps your creative process in huge ways. Self-acceptance and self-love allow you the safety net you need to explore and experiment. As Brené Brown said, "Vulnerability is the birthplace of innovation, creativity, and change." Being okay with all the parts of yourself lays the groundwork for your creative practice. Being open to sharing that tender stuff (vulnerable) takes you further into sharing your story. (See more about Brené Brown on page 62.)

THREE WAYS TO FIND YOUR CREATIVE SUBJECT

1. Internal (Soul Archaeology)

Dig through your unconscious self for images (content) to figure out what you want to say. Cultivate your own history and desire to find your subject. The story you are looking for isn't outside yourself. Use your experience, preferences, and tastes to guide you. It is my belief that by going far into your own heart you can find a deep connection to every living being. If you let yourself dig deep within your heart, you will see there a reflection of all humanity.

This method is a contemplative and process-oriented method that calls on you to be in the moment. This process can involve meditative reflection combined with drawing, sketching, or writing to catalog the voiceless part of your unconscious.

Photo by Dylan Sherwood McConnell

DYLAN SHERWOOD MCCONNELL IS AN ARTIST, MUSICIAN, AND FATHER LIVING IN NEVADA CITY, CALIFORNIA. HE USES HIS WHOLE LIFE AS HIS RAW MATERIAL. PARENTING, MUSIC, AND SCULPTURE ALL BLEND TOGETHER INTO ONE THING: A LIFE OF COMPLETE CREATIVITY. HIS WORK ISN'T LIMITED TO THIS THING OR THAT THING. HIS WORK IS HIS LIFE.

2. External (Research)

Pick a subject that interests you and research it. If you are interested in, say, Greek mythology, and particularly Athena, you might focus on one aspect of Athena and bring it to light through your creative expression. Use your interests as a starting point to launch an investigation. Sometimes creative people are more like scientists and researchers, delving into an idea to uncover the universal truth and beauty of human existence.

3. Catharsis

Catharsis is the spontaneous and healing creation of art that is born as you process your life and your emotions. Sometimes catharsis yields creations that aren't totally satisfying to the viewer, because they weren't made to be pretty—they were made to heal. Catharsis is an expression that is a form of art therapy.

MOST OF US USE SOME COMBINATION OF ALL THREE OF THESE METHODS AS WE MAKE THINGS.

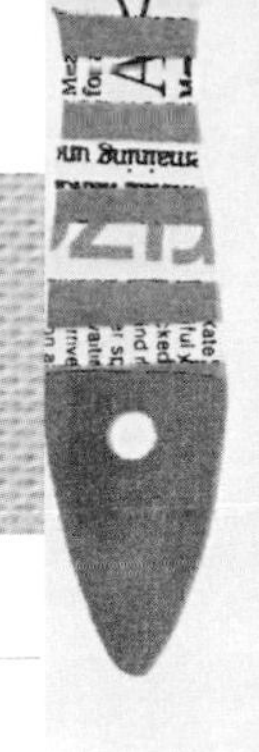

Make an Inventory of YOU

In this exercise, you'll create some starting points for you to use in your self-expression.

What do you want to say? What does it feel like to just be you, the complexity of you, the wholeness of you? What does it feel like in your bones and skin? What makes you come alive? What fires have you walked through that have made you who you are? These fires will light the path. In this activity, you'll make an inventory of the things that make you **you**. The answers are just for you. You'll see patterns in your answers as you uncover your true self.

On a separate sheet of paper, write down the following:

- Three of your most joyful experiences
- A painful experience
- Ten things for which you are grateful
- The kindest thing someone ever said to you or about you
- What makes you happier than anything else
- Something you have never told anyone
- Your all-time favorite five movies, books, and songs
- What you would create if you knew no one would judge you (be specific)
- The best dream you ever had in your life
- When you feel the most beautiful
- When you feel the most alive
- What makes you feel loved
- What you would grab if your house were on fire

This is a reflective exercise to help you find your voice. Just be with it. These answers are just for you. You don't need to do anything with them. If you are vulnerable enough, some of your life story may show up in your work. You might even use this list as source material for your creations.

SPARK

23

Repetition

JEREMY BRIDDELL IS ONE OF THE MOST TALENTED PEOPLE I KNOW. HE CAN WHIP OUT EXQUISITE POTS IN THE TIME IT TAKES ME TO BRUSH MY TEETH. HE SPEAKS IN CLAY AND HE IS FLUENT. BECAUSE OF HIS LONG RELATIONSHIP WITH HIS MATERIAL HE CAN COAX MANY LANGUAGES FROM HIS PIECES—FROM LOOSE, WABI-SABI TEA BOWLS TO TIGHTER GEOMETRIC FORMS.

A man was walking down the street in New York City. He asked directions from a passerby. "How do I get to Carnegie Hall?" The stranger replied, "Practice, practice, practice."

We get better at anything we try to do by doing it over and over (and over and over).

My pottery teacher, Jeremy Briddell, once told me, "Throw a hundred bowls and you'll begin to understand how to throw a bowl."

To the beginning potter, throwing one bowl can take an hour: centering the clay, coning it up, opening up the form, and so on. To the expert, this same bowl can be achieved within five minutes. The beginner is methodical, hesitant, careful, perfectionistic—she is trying hard to make it look good. The beginner is in love with the object and is set on winning the prize—catching the fish. She has little control of her movements or the object but still is trying so hard to control.

The expert has a fluency and fluidity with the materials and her movements. The expert understands the rhythm and harmony of the wheel, the clay, and her body. The expert can feel her way through the bowl instead of thinking her way through. The expert is cavalier and unattached to each bowl. She is unafraid to tell the clay exactly what to do, and she uses great economy of movement in the process. She is fully in control of her craft and yet chooses to surrender that control to the clay. She converses with the clay.

There is only one way to achieve the fluency, freedom, and grace of the expert, and that is by doing.

You don't learn by *thinking about doing*. You might enjoy thinking and planning, but the learning comes from doing. Each time the pottery student throws a bowl, a new awareness of the clay is born. And on and on it goes until the hundredth bowl and beyond.

The reality of the creative life, no matter what form your creativity takes, is that you will have to work. To do it well you need to keep going, work hard, and try.

We learn by coding the habit of creating into our body. Repetition is the key.

I highly recommend that when you sit down to throw a hundred bowls or sketch twenty self-portraits that you not go it alone. This depends on your learning style (take the quiz, page 98), but regardless, information is everywhere. If you aren't in a class or don't have a friend to ask, go online and watch a video. If you're getting stuck each time you try to center the clay, go ask the Internet, "How do I center clay on a wheel?" As you explore, seek out information and answers to your specific questions.

Do This

So what is your learning style? Take this fun quiz!

1. When you get a new piece of furniture from IKEA, you:

a. Carefully read the instruction manual and look at the diagrams, then start building

b. Ask someone you know to help you figure it out

c. Push the manual aside as you reach for your tools to start assembling

2. When you are on a scenic leaf-peeping road trip and you suddenly realize your cell phone, which contained the map app, died and you are lost, you:

a. Purchase a map at the first gas station you see

b. Ask the first person you see how to get back to the highway

c. Start driving and know that you'll figure it out by the road signs

3. When you are shopping in Costco and you see a salesperson demonstrating a new blender, you:

a. Pay close attention to her as she uses the machine, then ask to see the box so you can look at the pictures

b. Listen carefully to her words while trying to tune out that annoying loud whizzing sound

c. Ask if you can have a turn trying it out for yourself

4. When it's time to plant the annual summer garden, you:

a. Pore over plant seed catalogs, magazines, and gardening books to get inspired

b. Call your gardener friend and chat about what worked and what didn't work in her garden last year

c. Head to the garden center to pick out a bunch of plants, mulch, and seeds and then dig in

5. It is time to host your favorite cool new friends for dinner—and they are foodies! You:

a. Grab your best cookbooks and start dog-earing pages, and then go online to research more recipes from your favorite chefs

b. Talk to your fishmonger to get advice about which fish to serve

c. Just head into the kitchen and start playing with your haul from the farmers' market

6. You have a big deadline coming up and are feeling a bit stressed. You need to figure out how to finish all your work and so you need a plan. You:

a. Write it all down on a piece of paper as a list, then maybe make a flowchart or timeline or calendar to help you set your goals

b. Seek advice from a friend and then repeat the steps in your mind until you feel comfortable

c. Say, "Deadlines, schmeadlines! Who cares?" You are just going to start working and trust that you will get it all done in time

Tally up your answers to find your score.

a. If you answered mostly **a**, then you are a *visual learner*. You have to see it to get it! You want to be shown. You want charts, pictures, books, illustrations, maps, video tutorials, diagrams, and demos. You learn through observing the world with your eyes. If your teacher shows you something, you will watch her and then emulate her with your body until you understand.

b. If you answered mostly **b**, you are an *auditory learner*. You love a good lecture! You like to listen, chat, talk, share, and hear what others are saying. You love listening to your teacher's words, and you can understand it if someone says it to you rather than if someone shows you. Sometimes you talk to yourself to absorb the information by saying it out loud. It helps you learn.

c. If you answered mostly **c**, you are a *tactile/kinesthetic learner*. You aren't going to stop to read a manual! You won't be happy until you dig right in and get your hands dirty. You learn by doing it for yourself. You may make mistakes, but you will learn from them. You are going to figure it out. You have little patience for long-winded explanations because you just want to get going!

Now that you know your learning style, use it to help you as you explore, study, try new things, and create.

SPARK

24

Shine Your Light

JEWELRY DESIGNER LOGAN MILLIKEN STARTED HER COMPANY, SILVER & SAGE, IN SCOTTSDALE, ARIZONA, WITH NOTHING BUT A DREAM. THE MORE SHE MADE, THE MORE PEOPLE SHE ATTRACTED. LOGAN SHINES HER LIGHT THROUGH HER EXQUISITE, COLORFUL JEWELRY. SHE HAS NOW OUTGROWN ONE SMALL STUDIO AND IS STILL GROWING. LOGAN IS A BEACON. THE LIGHT IN HER HEART TOUCHES PEOPLE THROUGH HER CREATIONS.

"Burn like a good bonfire in whatever you do."

FROM THE SONG "BONFIRE" BY ANDREW JOHN BARLOW AND LOUISE ANN RHODES OF THE BAND LAMB

Do you play a shell game with your inner glow? Do you in some ways feel unworthy of the great beacon that lives inside your heart? At the same time, how easy is it for you to help support your children, friends, or spouse to shine their light? Pretty easy to help someone else, isn't it?

We are trained by our culture to be humble, not arrogant or prideful—which is good. But we can easily confuse the idea of being proud or attention seeking with shining our light. It may feel awkward or uncomfortable to shine when we are commonly applauded for tempering our ego and going with the flow, fitting in and not being too loud. We are conditioned to know how to have a place in the group—in our family, in the community, at school, and at work.

You may need to get a bit more comfortable putting yourself out there, because you are probably going to have to share your creations with the world. Hence, you've got to shine your light. It isn't arrogant, egocentric, or attention seeking to shine out from your heart. It is more like becoming a beacon. The more you reach inside for your passion and potential, the more other people will see and feel that in you. They will comment on it. You will inspire them. You may be part of someone else's creative journey.

I HEREBY OFFICIALLY GRANT YOU PERMISSION TO SHINE YOUR LIGHT.

Don't diminish your glow for anyone else or for any reason—ever. Some of your friends or family might project negative feelings onto you as you pursue your creativity. Perhaps you will feel it in teasing remarks that aren't really funny. That is their issue, not yours.

Your passion belongs to you. No one can take it away. Don't feel bad about your joy. Don't make excuses for it to make a friend feel more comfortable about herself. That isn't modesty or humility—that's diminishing your glow.

My mom taught me about this when I was young. I didn't get it when I was a teenager in high school. I was typically hyper-focused on my perceived shortcomings. I was zoomed in, myopic, scrutinizing my every flaw.

> My mom would say to me: "You have to love you." No one else can love you if you don't love you. If you love yourself, then people will understand that they have permission to love you, too.

It took me a few years, but I got it, and I am so grateful to my mom for that teaching.

As you have already read, so much of creativity has to do with something much greater than just making pretty things. You have to let go of the feeling that you don't deserve to be happy or that you could never have the freedom that you seek.

Being comfortable inside your skin is a life's work. It has its merits. Let's say you want to show your paintings in a gallery, or take your web design business to the next level with clients, or pitch your first book. You will need to practice confidence and allow yourself and others to see the light in your heart. You may as well start now.

Love and accept yourself right now. Feel good about even tiny accomplishments: you finished your tenth self-portrait or you put a binding on a quilt. **Celebrate your small victories.** Pat yourself on the back. Know that we are all just practicing at everything we do. That is one of the words I love most about yoga. We say we *practice* yoga. We should say we *practice* everything. Practicing is the only truth. Parenting is a practice. Our work at the office is a practice. We practice all the time.

And so, shining your light is a practice. Your creative process is a practice. Believing in yourself is a practice. The more you practice, the better you get. And the more you practice, the more able you are to accept your limitations and shortcomings, because there is always another chance to try again, to do it differently and maybe better.

Celebrate yourself. Celebrate each step. Sparkle. Today and this week, treat yourself with the same kindness, gentleness, and love that you would show to your dear friend or child.

shine
& loVe
BLESSINGS
"Let the beauty of what you do." –Rumi
be who you are.
LOVE
Look for
your
light

SPARK

25

Make a SoulBox

HOLLY TOOK MY SOULBOX WORKSHOP AND FILLED HER BOX WITH MEANINGFUL IMAGES OF HER FAMILY. WHEN SHE WENT HOME, HER THREE KIDS COULDN'T WAIT TO MAKE BOXES OF THEIR OWN. THESE ARE THEIR CREATIONS. THIS IS A GREAT ACTIVITY TO SHARE WITH FRIENDS AND FAMILY.

A SoulBox is a project I cooked up that lets you do a bit of soul archaeology and have fun while making a meaningful reminder of what is most important to you. It will remind you of your passion. You can use it as a resource when you need it. It is a special place for gathering meaningful things, words, and ideas. Essentially, it is a decorated box, filled with messages, images, and treasures (found or made).

IT WILL REMIND YOU OF YOUR PASSION.

A poignant episode of *The Simpsons* showed Marge Simpson in her bedroom. Her daughter, Lisa, was peering into her mom's closet and noticed a box on a high shelf. She asked what it was. Marge replied, "Oh, that's just my box of broken dreams." She pulled it down and showed Lisa her old ballet shoes and remnants of a life she never pursued. I know you can relate to that. I did. Get out your box from the closet and open it up. The SoulBox is your answer to Marge's box of broken dreams.

Your box might be filled with gratitude or affirmations. It might contain remnants from your past and your childhood dreams. You can write down each of your blessings from Count Your Blessings (page 35) on cut rectangles of card stock and use it as a blessings bank, adding more and more slips of paper until it is overflowing.

Do This

Make a SoulBox

WHAT YOU NEED

- Empty wooden cigar box (you can often get these at cigar or smoke shops); you can also use a tin, a shoe box, or any other box you have around
- Materials from around your house: photos, trinkets, objects, or crafting items
- Pretty art papers, decorative paper, or gold leaf to cover the inside or outside of the box
- Card stock
- Special crafty stuff that you have been holding on to for a long time and you aren't sure what to do with—you were saving it for this!
- Natural materials from outside, such as seashells or branches (if you are so inclined)
- Paste, glue, glue gun, Mod Podge, tape
- Acrylic paints and brushes
- Magazines to find images and words
- Craft knife (such as X-ACTO) and/or scissors

WHAT TO DO

You may want to invite a few friends over when you do this so you can all make boxes, or maybe you want to work alone. Assemble your desired materials. Look at the treasures you have collected. Maybe you have a plan in your mind and you go for it, or maybe you just start doing things to your box and see where it takes you. As you are working, don't fret about whether it is perfect or even pretty. Just let it be playful and meaningful to you.

Decide how you want to treat the surface of the box. Maybe covered in paper? Use Mod Podge, matte medium, or paste to decoupage the decorative papers to the surfaces of your box. The outside and inside might be completely different. Let the box dry; then add any embellishments you want. After it is completely decorated, start filling it with treasures, pictures, words on cards—anything!

Place your box next to your bed or somewhere you can see it daily. Let it be a changing space—add to it; take things out. Have a conversation with yourself through your box.

I lead SoulBox workshops and everyone makes something special and unique. One friend chose a plain, flat cigar box and decorated it with Japanese paper. She used hot glue to attach a heart-shaped rock to the top. Inside, she put three wedding pictures.

I asked her about her lovely, simple box and she said, "My husband and I are working through some things. We aren't as connected as I wish we were. Things aren't bad, but they could be better. This box is a place for us to leave each other notes and to communicate." I was amazed by her creativity and how she made the box a special space to use as a romantic mailbox. Later, I followed up with her and she told me that she and her husband use it all the time, even leaving gifts and "I'm sorry" notes. My friend Elaina turned hers into a jewelry box so she can use it every day.

SPARK 26

Take a Day Off

Sometimes you've got to go find your soul on the road.

I am not one of those people who would ever tell anyone to get into their studio no matter what and sit there and move their hands until the creative spirit strikes. There are other books for that. There are books that tell you to be orderly and disciplined as you pursue your passion, to treat it like a job, to punch in on the time clock, to be diligent and earnest in your efforts—constant, consistent, patient. These books want you to sit around in the studio and wait until a butterfly flies into the room. Precisely because you have been in there waiting, you will be ready for it. It's sort of like fishing for magic—if you wait long enough, something wonderful will happen.

Then again, you could just take the day off—actually go fishing, connect with the natural world and your senses—and come back filled with inspiration and magic, ready to get to work. Personally, I'll go with the second option any day.

I must add that part of me wants to be that sort of disciplined person, the person who goes into her studio in an orderly, disciplined routine, with consistency and regularity. I really do. And you might be. But I'm not.

You can't get blood from a stone. Or is it a turnip?

I picture the alchemist holed up for hours, tinkering and toying, hunching and hiding, waiting to make gold. This is a noble pursuit. And this may work for you. But sometimes you've got to go find your soul on the road, or in a book, or at the beach. You've got to

LAURA KRAMER'S INCREDIBLE NATURE-INSPIRED GLASS ART.

run away and do nothing. I'd much rather not work and go fill up on popcorn at a French film, or take a road trip to a nearby town, than sit around waiting for my spirit to fly into the room—waiting for magic. You can't force your creativity. You can't strong-arm your inspiration. I do believe in waiting it out.

Don't get me wrong. I also believe in working. I believe in working through the boredom, the obstacles, the writer's block. But there is a time and a place for everything. Sometimes you just have to run away. Sometimes you need time to recharge the battery. Sometimes you need to play hooky. Then, when you come back to your work you are so much more relaxed, and more often than not you have gotten past your roadblock and are able to see abundance, blessings, and inspiration all around you. This stuff is source for the Spark. For me, inspiration lies in the world, everywhere—love, passion, family, relationship, connection, and kindness. This is what I use as raw material. I can't always get in touch with the source of my creativity when I'm cooped up in my cinder-block studio. I have to go be in the world and jog my senses to find it. I have to ignite the flame by playing and looking and exploring the world.

You can't force your creativity.

YOU CAN'T STRONG-ARM YOUR INSPIRATION.

LAURA KRAMER IS A MANIPULATOR OF THE NATURAL AND HANDMADE—A GLASSMAKER, TRAVELER, AND ARCHAEOLOGIST—WHO LIVES BY THE BEACH IN RHODE ISLAND WITH HER SON, FIN.

Do This

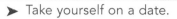

- Take yourself on a date.
- Get thee to the museum, the concert, the bakery, the glassblowing demo, the poetry slam.
- Go find something new. Google it. Research it. Go find it. Travel to see it.
- Go watch an expert pursuing her craft—you learn so much by watching subtle movements and seeing small technical tricks.
- If you schedule it on your calendar like a date with a friend, you'll definitely show up. Show up for yourself. Enjoy your company.

Photos by Asya Palatova

SPARK 27

Share Your Work

WE LOVE LEMONADE STANDS AROUND HERE. THE LEMONADE STAND REPRESENTS ALL THE BEST QUALITIES OF CAPITALISM: DIY GUMPTION, SIMPLE TRANSACTIONS, CONNECTION, AND SELF-EMPOWERED SHARING—TAKING IT TO THE STREETS!

TAKE IT TO THE STREET

There are basically two ways to share your creations with the world. The first is the traditional face-to-face sharing of the gallery show, the craft fair, or the concert. You might invite a few friends over to show them what you've been up to. These days, businesses want to feature local artisans, so talk to shop owners about featuring your wares. Approach a local coffee house or boutique about using its walls for a month.

Artist Marcel Duchamp believed that his work wasn't finished until it was seen by people—that the viewing completed the work. I love that.

For me, there is no greater or more connected form of commerce than the lemonade stand. It is the perfect model for small business. The lemonade stand is the perfect representation of belief in oneself.

Photo by Carrie Bloomston

When you are ready to sell your stuff, think of it as a lemonade stand. You want to make more money than you spend, but at first your investment in materials (lemons and sugar) may be greater than your profits.

Local farmers' markets and craft fairs are a great way for you to start. There is usually no contract or commitment, and fees are low. You show up, make a pretty display, and open up your lemonade stand! As for taking in money in an easy way, get a card reader for your phone (squareup.com) to accept credit cards on the spot. The market will let you know where to register your business for local tax purposes.

Finally, there are more and more sites on the web that allow you to set up your very own online retail shop, such as Etsy. They are simple to use and you don't need to have a separate website plus additional shopping cart functionality.

BLOG ABOUT IT

The second way to share is via social media. The amazingly vibrant modern craft movement happening around the world is borne aloft on the wings of Twitter, Instagram, Facebook, Pinterest, blogs, and more. Social media allow you to share your process through photos as well as keeping all your friends in the loop.

Blogging is a way to give voice to your process. And there are a million voices out there. Just know that the only person really reading your blog is your mom. Seriously. Do it for you, not for the implied reader. Use a blog platform like Blogger or Wordpress to create your blog when you are ready.

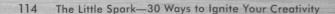

PRESENTATION IS EVERYTHING

If I had to distill my entire four years of fancy art education into one sentence, it would be this: Presentation is everything. Regardless of how you choose to share your work, this is the key. (I just saved you a lot of money and four years.) The clearer, more precise, and more intentional you are about your presentation, the better your viewer will be able to see your work.

If you make beautiful abstract paintings in your studio for six months but have a show in a grungy, poorly lit bar behind a pool table, then you aren't doing yourself any favors.

You want to set the stage for the viewer. Beginning with the graphic design of your show announcement, you are telling a story about yourself and your process. People will see your love. They will see and appreciate your work that much more if you have filled the gallery with fragrant stargazer lilies and mopped the floor with eucalyptus oil. They might not even be aware of all the preparations, scents, cleaning, graphic design, and work you have done, but it will help your work. Whatever the tone you are trying to set, set it fully. Go all the way.

Do This

How would you like to share your work?

- Write down some ideas here. Research your options. Contact people at local farmers' markets, craft fairs, coffee shops, or galleries. Check out blog platforms and maybe design your own blog. If you are a writer, submit your work to your favorite online or print journal. Whatever it is and however you choose, get out there and start sharing your work. Make your own lemonade stand!

SPARK

28

Give It Away

LONDON-BASED FASHION DESIGNER HOLLY DUNLAP IS CHANGING THE WORLD. HER COMPANY, MAKONO, EMPLOYS DISABLED WORKERS TO PRODUCE GOODS AT HER FACTORY IN MALAWI, AFRICA. HER DESIGNS REFLECT REGIONAL CRAFTS WITH A HIGH-FASHION SPIN. HOLLY LETS HER DESIRE TO GIVE BACK AND HEAL THE WORLD LIGHT HER BUSINESS PATH. BUT HER GLOW LIGHTS THE PATH FOR ALL OF US TO GIVE BACK EVEN IN MODEST WAYS.

Photos by Jenny Dawson

"Find love, then give it all away."

CLEM SNIDE

As you have learned in this book, creativity is a way of being—a way of thinking, living, and expressing. It isn't limited to art or even to something we make. It is a way of releasing the contents of the human heart. We find love; then we give it all away.

I have so many friends, mothers my age, who tell me they aren't creative but they wish they were. They organize their families and their homes, and they fill up bento boxes with colorful, nutritious lunches every day. Often, they give their time to charities—organizing the gala or school auction. I look at them, mystified by their inability to see their own gifts, and say, "But you organized that entire auction, from top to bottom, and a hundred people, and all those gift baskets!" The light goes on when I say this. They can see that it is a very creative act.

Parenting is without a doubt the most creative thing I have ever done. It calls for openheartedness from moment to moment. It challenges my previous notions and ideas about almost everything. It requires me to think in new ways to best serve the needs and wants of my family and my children. It asks me to say **yes** instead of **no**. Often, as moms to young children, we are tired. Kids don't know what that means. They just go-go-go! We have to find resources (creativity) to get everyone's needs met. When my kids were babies I was very aware that saying **no** was often way easier than saying **yes**. I realized that **no** is not about the child, but about the parent. **No** comes from a failure of the imagination. **No** comes from fatigue, mediocrity, status quo, and knee-jerk reactions. **No** is certainly easier, but the child misses out. That's why I said **yes** and still do.

Today was a bright November day in Arizona. My kids wanted to throw the football in the neighbor's grassy yard, and I didn't want to say no again. So I folded the week's laundry in the driveway—a creative solution (albeit a bit kooky), and everyone was happy. These are the little choices we make every day that add up to a much bigger picture—a happy family picture.

Photo by Kris Keu

There are so many ways you can be creative when you are called upon: You step up to bat so easily when it is for someone or something else—your kids, the school auction, your friends, your spouse or partner, your family, or your church or community. This is a generosity of spirit.

In yoga, at the very end of class, when it is time to do the most challenging back bend, my teacher, Anton Mackey, will often say, "Do this backbend as if it is for someone else.

➤ List a few ways in which you are already creative in your daily life:

Think of someone right now who doesn't have the ability to move or breathe the way you are right now. Think of that person, and do this for them." That is a profound teaching. Give it away. Give it to someone else and you will be able to access the best in you.

We are often able to rise to our highest self if it is for someone else. Now that you are on your creative path, you might find that you have opportunities to use your expression to give back—to help others.

When you are in your creative process, you'll end up with a lot of things that you have made. It feels good to come full circle and let go of some of it.

Do you make jewelry? I bet you'll have ten pairs of earrings by the time you are finished with your jewelry class. What to do with them? Give them away. Go to a women's shelter and offer up your gifts. Donate your work to the school auction.

Are you throwing ceramic bowls? There is a great national charity called Empty Bowls. Empty Bowls brings together potters, other craftspeople, educators, and people who work with the community to create handcrafted bowls. Guests are invited to a simple meal of soup and bread. In exchange for a cash donation, the guests are asked to keep a bowl as a reminder of all the empty bowls in the world. The money raised is donated to an organization working to end hunger.

Do This

Now that you have found your love, your creativity, your Spark, it may help to remember to give it away. Let the light shine out and touch other people. Using your gifts to help others is a nourishing experience. You'll get back way more than you'll give.

- How can you use the gifts of your Spark to give? Whom can you give your creations to?

SPARK

29

Leave It on the Field

THIS QUOTE IS WRITTEN ON THE FLOOR OF KALEIDOSCOPE JUICE. WHEN THE BUSINESS WAS YOUNG AND GROWING, THE OWNER, ALEXANDRA, HAD TO MAKE A BIG DECISION: PAY THE UTILITY BILL OR BUY A NEW JUICER. ALEXANDRA SAID, "I GUESS I'LL JUST LEAP AND A NET WILL APPEAR." HER FRIEND DUSTI REPLIED, "NO, LEAP AND YOUR WINGS WILL APPEAR!" SOMETIMES YOU HAVE TO DO MORE THAN HOPE AGAINST FEAR. YOU HAVE TO STEP INTO GRACE AND FLY. HOW CREATIVE TO PAINT HER INSPIRATION ON THE FLOOR! TALK ABOUT STANDING IN YOUR TRUTH.

Said the soccer coach to my son's second-grade soccer team: "I am proud of what you did out there. You did your best. You left it all on the field."

Leave it on the field. Make yourself proud. Give it your all. Do your best. Don't hold back, waiting for some special moment to shine your brightest. Right now is when you should shine. Right now is when you step up into the fullness of your potential. Leave it on the field. Leave it in the dance, on the canvas, in the pie, in the clay, in the song. Know that you can and you will.

RIGHT NOW IS WHEN YOU SHOULD SHINE.

I used to think I had to save it all up for this or that. I used to be all boxed in and compartmentalized. I would reserve parts of myself to be shared and doled out here and there as I saw fit. I shared some of me with some people and other parts of me with other people. Some knew me as a mom, some as an artist, some as a spiritual seeker, some as a knitter, a glassblower, a painter, a designer … I finally let go of that a few years ago when I began the process of letting go of control. I am in recovery from control—control over others, myself, my thoughts, my life, my reality, the outcome, and my image.

When you let go of control, you surrender to life and all its beauty and blessings. You can't force your creativity into existence. Creativity is more like water. It flows. You get to catch it for a few minutes in your hands before it spills out and moves on, so you engage with it in a way that calls on you to let go, to flow, to be present. You have to let go of expectations and just deal with what you find in the moment.

Maybe today I expect to finish that one painting that has eluded me. But maybe I get into my studio and all I make is a mess of it. Maybe I sit down to sew, and for some reason that one corner of the patchwork just won't lie flat and it keeps slipping and I keep ripping it out until the cotton shreds. That happens. Befriend incidents, accidents, and mishaps. They are your greatest teachers.

No matter what form your creativity takes, you have to let go of expectation and perfection. For the record, **there is no such thing as perfect**. I tell this to my students, my children, and myself. And even if there were, would you want it? Think of it this way: if you ever finally made the perfect quilt or painting or cake, you'd never need to make another one, right? Your desire would be extinguished and you'd sit and stare forever at your creation in the mirror, like Narcissus. Eventually, you'd fall face first into that reflection and that would be that.

There is no such thing as perfection. There is only trying, doing your best, and leaving it all on the field. If you do your best, honor your journey, and love yourself along the way, then you will find the pot of gold at the end of your rainbow. The pot of gold is everywhere when you go with the flow, surrender to the process, stop controlling, and let yourself be filled with joy and love. For me, that is the point of my creative practice. It fills me with an ebullient spirit that brightens the rest of my life. When we share our work, vision, ideas, and love with others, we get just as much as we give.

CREATIVITY IS NOT SOMETHING YOU DO; IT IS WHO YOU ARE.

I hope that as I parent my children and make dinner and drive carpool I am as creative in my heart and mind as I am when I am being a writer or an artist. You are one person with many impulses and urges. You can reveal your truth to as many or as few people as you want, but your gifts will touch others if you let yourself be vulnerable enough to share.

Through this book, you have learned many things about yourself. You have learned a few of the mechanical aspects of creativity, such as finding your creative time of day and how to make your creative space. You have uncovered a few things about yourself and your past that have blanketed and hidden your creativity from you, and you have begun to let them go. You have learned about how to present and share your work and shine your light. I hope you have learned that no matter what, you are good enough exactly as you are right now, and your life experience will fill your work with your spirit.

Do This

It is your turn to step into the greatness of yourself and your creativity. Go play. Have fun. Make messes. Share yourself and your vision. Be who you are. Do your best. Leave it on the field.

SPARK

30

Trust Yourself

Now that you have read this book, let me tell you one last thing to take with you on your adventure:

NOTHING YOU NEED TO KNOW IS IN THIS BOOK OR ANY OTHER.

Nothing you need is in a class or at the museum or at the art supply store. Everything you need is within you. After all, you were born with it. Trust your intuition. Let it guide you. Trust your inner knowing and your gut. The little Spark will take you where you need to go. Just listen to it. Follow it. Trust it. Trust yourself and you will awaken to the potential inside you. You already have everything you need.

TRUST yourself. trust yourself. TRUST YOURSELF.
URSELF. Trust yourself trust yourself. TRUST you
t yourself! Trust Yourself Trust yourself. Trust you
ust your self. Trust Yourself. Trus
UST YOURSELF. TRUST YOURSELF. TRUST yourself. trust yourse
OURSELF! TRUST Yourself. TRUST YOURSELF. trust Yourself. T
ust yourself TRUST YOURSELF. TRU
urself. trust yourself. TRUST YOURSELF. TRUST YOURSELF.
TRUST yourself. TRUST yourself. trust yourself. trust you
ust yourself. TRUST yourself. trust yourself. trust
ust YOURSelf. T.R.U.S.T. Yourself. Trust Yourself. trust yo
TRUST yourself. trust yourself. Trust yourself.
TRUST YOURSELF. TRUST YOURSE
ust yourself. trust yourself. trust YOURself. trust YOU
ourself. TRUST YOURSELF. TRUST YOURSELF. trust
ust yourself. Trust yourself. trust yourself. TRUST YOURS
urself. TRUST YOURSELF. trust yourself. Trust yourself
ust yourself. Trust yourself. Trust yourself. TRUST YOURSE
TRUST yourself. trust yourself. trust
RUST OURSELF
trust yourself. TRUST YOURSELF. TRUS
T.R.U.S.T. YOURSELF trust yourself.
yourself. trust yourself. TRUST YOURSELF.
Trust yourself. trust yourself. trust yourself
self. trust yourself. TRUST YOURSELF. TRUST. TRUST
trust yourself. trust yourself. trust yourself. Tru
yourself. TRUST YOURSELF. trust yourself. Trust you
Trust yourself. trust yourself. I TRUST YOU.
Trust yourself. T.R.U.S.T. trust yourself. TRUST YO
self. TRUST YOURSELF. TRUST YOURSelf.
ST YOURSELF. Trust your
ust yourself. trust yourself
ourself. Trust yourself. Trust yourself. TRUST YOURSE

Contributors

BARI ACKERMAN p. 50 textile designer
Scottsdale, Arizona • barijdesigns.com

DOUG BAULOS p. 68
artist • Birmingham, Alabama
machinewithnoname.blogspot.com

CHRIS BIANCO p. 86 chef/restaurateur
Phoenix, Arizona • pizzeriabianco.com

JEREMY BRIDDELL pp. 42, 96, 97
potter and ceramic artist
Phoenix, Arizona • jeremybriddell.com

CYNDI COON pp. 12, 27, 32, 73, 81, 83
artist and art journaler
Tempe, Arizona • laboratory5.com

HOLLY DUNLAP p. 116 fashion designer
Malawi, Africa/London, UK • makono.com

FANCY TIGER CRAFTS p. 16
fabric and yarn store
Denver, Colorado • fancytiger.com

SHELLY FIGUEROA pp. 13, 17
sewing pattern designer
Lake Oswego, Oregon • figgyspatterns.com

SHEA HENDERSON p. 14
sewing pattern designer
Kansas City, Missouri
emptybobbinsewing.com

SCOTTY JOHNSON p. 64
guitarist for Gin Blossoms and Honey Girl
Phoenix, Arizona • ginblossoms.net and honeygirlmusic.com

LAURA KRAMER pp. 109, 111
glassblower and artist
Providence, Rhode Island • lbkstudio.com

ANTON MACKEY pp. 56, 57, 118
yoga teacher
Scottsdale, Arizona • antonyoga.com

ALEXANDRA MAW pp. 53, 84, 121
owner of Kaleidoscope Juice
Phoenix, Arizona • kaleidoscopejuice.com

DYLAN SHERWOOD MCCONNELL pp. 8, 94
artist • Nevada City, California
dsmcconnell.com

LOGAN MILLIKEN pp. 67, 72, 100
jewelry designer and owner of Silver & Sage
Scottsdale, Arizona • silverandsagejewelry.com

ADAM RAYMONT p. 72
artist • Berlin, Germany and Brooklyn, New York • adamraymontstudio.com

SUSAN SILVERMAN pp. 40, 91
dancer and dance instructor
Phoenix, Arizona • dancetheaterwest.com

KIKI SMITH p. 15 artist
New York, New York • pacegallery.com

AYUMI TAKAHASHI p. 36
sewing pattern designer
Tokyo, Japan • ayumills.blogspot.com

About the Author

When Carrie was two, her mom found her all tangled up in the needlepoint yarn and knew Carrie would be an artist. Her creative mom loved to paint and craft and later became an interior designer. Her savvy designer dad still designs and manufactures clothing. Carrie's parents held her tiny artist Spark in their hands and protected it from the wind. That makes her lucky.

Carrie studied painting and glassblowing at the Rhode Island School of Design and spent the next decade recovering from it.

She dreamed big, moved to New York, outgrew her dream, and went back home to the desert to get married. She and her husband owned a decorative arts business for 17 years, and she continued to make art. She became a mom and then learned with the help of her children, finally, how to become who she always wanted to be: herself. She learned that who she is is who she always was: the same teenage girl who painted big abstract pieces about the beauty of this life on her floor. She aims to help you become yourself, too.

Now a professional artist, textile designer, abstract painter, writer, and teacher, Carrie lives in a happy home with her about-to-be-a-therapist husband and loves being a mother to two sparkly and inspiring kids. Her children light her way. She holds their little Sparks in her hand, protecting them from the wind.

Follow Carrie via her website and blog: such-designs.com.

A FEW OF CARRIE'S MUST-READ BOOKS

Writing Down the Bones by Natalie Goldberg

Zen Mind, Beginner's Mind by Shunryu Suzuki

Drawing on the Right Side of the Brain by Betty Edwards

The Pink Refrigerator by Tim Egan

Any of Jalaluddin Rumi's poetry, translated by Coleman Barks

The Gifts of Imperfection by Brené Brown

Octavio Paz Selected Poems by Octavio Paz

Anything by Pema Chodron, especially *Start Where You Are*, *Getting Unstuck*, and *Don't Bite the Hook*

Anything by Marianne Williamson, especially *A Return to Love*

HER MUST-WATCH MOVIES

Ratatouille

Searching for Bobby Fischer

Amadeus

Big Night

Up

Jiro Dreams of Sushi

Mostly Martha

Frida

The Matrix

The Secret Life of Walter Mitty

My Left Foot

Strictly Ballroom

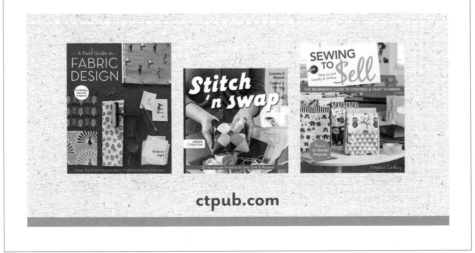